Straight Talk With Kids

Straight Talk with Kids:

Improving Communication, Building Trust, and Keeping Your Children Drug Free

The Scott Newman Center

with the assistance of Beth Anne
Munger, M.S., substance abuse
prevention program coordinator,
Palos Verdes Peninsula Unified
School District

BANTAM BOOKS
NEW YORK · TORONTO · LONDON · SYDNEY · AUCKLAND

STRAIGHT TALK WITH KIDS

A Bantam Book / August 1991

Published by arrangement with the author

All rights reserved.
Copyright © 1991 by The Scott Newman Center.
Interior illustrations copyright © 1991 by Gil Asbby.
Book design by Beth Tondreau Design.
No part of this book may be reproduced or transmitted
in any form or by any means, electronic or mechanical,
including photocopying, recording, or by any information
storage and retrieval system, without permission in writing from
the publisher.
For information address: Bantam Books.

ISBN 0-553-29352-4

Published simultaneously in the United States and Canada

PRINTED IN THE UNITED STATES OF AMERICA

OPM 0 9 8 7 6 5 4 3 2 1

Parenting today is one of *the* most difficult jobs one can have in a lifetime, far more difficult than in generations past. In this rapidly changing world, kids face pressures and temptations that most of us never had to cope with.

They are bombarded on a daily basis with conflicting messages from role models, television, MTV, and print ads. With the increasing number of single parent families, combined families, and working mothers, the traditional American family structure appears to be a thing of the past. These factors, combined with the easy accessibility to chemical substances of all kinds, provide some serious obstacles along the road to adulthood.

We hope this book will provide you with some useful guidelines to help you relax a little and enjoy your role as a parent and to raise kids that grow up and remain drug free.

—Paul Newman and Joanne Woodward

CONTENTS

Straight Talk with Kids

Kids at Risk in a Drug-Filled World

Never before have concerned parents felt quite so helpless about the world they're trying to prepare their children for—and never before has that worry focused so strongly on drug use. Everyone has heard and read that alcohol and other drug use among teenagers in the United States is epidemic. National studies show that drug use among high-school students is greater in the United States than anywhere else in the industrialized world. News magazines feature stories about how cheap drugs have become, how openly they are sold. TV specials chronicle the unchecked flow of drugs across our country's borders. Most people know a neighbor or relative whose children have succumbed to the seduction of alcohol or other drugs; others know the threat exists but can't believe it could happen to their sons and daughters.

There are no absolute rules or magic formulas parents can follow to keep their children drug free. Parents must arm themselves with information about drugs as well as knowledge about their own child's needs. This book is meant to serve as a guide, *not* as a place to find easy solutions to your problems or absolute answers to your questions. The following chapters offer basic principles that professionals and parents have found useful in helping kids to find the strength and resources within themselves to cope with the confusing world around them.

PART ONE

Prevention

CHAPTER I

Building Strong Kids

ADOLESCENT REALITIES

Many adults often seem to forget, rewrite, or romanticize their own youth. It's easy for a busy person to become out of touch with the inner world of childhood and adolescence. Sometimes adults don't even notice that they often trivialize their children's problems or relegate them to secondary status. Because of the stress and strain of everyday life, parents find themselves falling into a kind of unconscious self-centeredness.

This is not an atypical scenario: Things at work may be tough. You are tired, angry, maybe a bit depressed at the end of a hard day or a hard week. There are bills to pay, a messy house to clean, food to buy, laundry to do. Maybe you would rather sit down, have a cup of coffee or a glass of wine, watch your favorite TV show instead of listening to your kids or asking them what their day was like. What could be so hard about going to school every day, doing a little homework, hanging out with friends, even working that part-time job? You begin to think that adult problems are more important and more difficult than the ones kids have. It is easy to forget that even if your job, for example, is a nightmare, you have acquired certain skills and mechanisms for coping. A thirteen-year-old or even a seventeen-year-old child has not had time to cultivate those skills.

Parents have a responsibility to teach, guide, and demonstrate to their children how to successfully navigate through life's often turbulent and stormy waters. It is not as though challenges and difficulties will cease for the adolescent once the teen years are over. It's not only between the ages of ten and eighteen that a person can feel confused, frustrated, bored, anxious, depressed, and misunderstood. Adults can certainly attest to the fact that the problems of life do not go away just by "growing up." Adolescence is just the beginning of facing life's problems, a time of preparation for an adulthood that will bring more complex and complicated challenges and temptations.

PARENTS should not underestimate the tremendous physical, intellectual, and psychological changes their adolescents are dealing with. These changes bring about an intense awareness of and often confusion about the new and different expectations from self and others. As teenagers ask questions they have never thought to ask before, they are struggling, often painfully, to redefine their relationships to themselves, to those in authority—especially their parents—and to members of the opposite sex.

In some sense, the adolescent feels estranged from the child she or he used to be, *and* from the adult she or he is one day expected to be. The result can be increased self-consciousness, greater self-scrutiny, and intense self-absorption, visible in many ways: in preoccupation with appearance, for example; in a move away from dependence on parental guidance; in an almost reflexive opposition to anything someone of the older generation might say. In short, those hours in front of the mirror are the signs of a person trying hard to get used to a new self, inside and out.

How parents handle this period can depend as much on their attitudes as on their skills. Psychologists have found that parents who approach their child's teen years thinking the challenge will be fun and interesting and who look forward to their child's growing independence have much better relationships with their kids than those who dread the changes. Some parents enjoy seeing their children mature and grow into more adult responsibilities. Others see their child's growing independence as a loss or threat to their authority.

It is of crucial importance that parents see their kids for who they are and what they are going through *now,* not how they might want or expect them to be in the future. Adolescents should not be seen as pre-adults, pre-workers, or pre-parents but as people developing and struggling for their identity under particular personal and historical circumstances.

Teenagers are human beings. Their struggle to separate from parents and establish their own identity must be respected. Parents should take the feelings and opinions of their children seriously and recognize that anxiety about a changing body, developing sexuality, and the future can cause a lot of stress and strain. Teenaged kids who are feeling betwixt and between want independence *and* security (as adults do too), freedom *and* limits. It is up to parents—and others in the older generation—to find the balance between these two extremes.

Parents should seek ways in which to help their children develop self-esteem and discover their own strengths and values through real and responsible participation in the world they live in. Kids need guidance that will enable them to cope with life's problems and make decisions

responsibly. Exploration and experimentation are necessary to the healthy growth of all human beings. How can parents provide an environment that encourages children to experiment and explore creatively and without damaging consequences?

FOSTERING OPEN COMMUNICATION

Giving kids time and attention means giving them your ear. It means listening and communicating. Young people need to know that they are seen and heard. *A child who is heard is a child who will listen*. Don't assume that your child will immediately confide in you. Learn to listen and even read between the lines. Try to know as much as you can about your child's moods.

To stay in touch with your child, it is important to make real conversations a part of your everyday living together. This means telling your child what is going on in your life—what you think about, your problems, concerns, and joys. Encourage your child to do the same. By sharing experiences from your own adolescence as well as your everyday life, you will help your child feel more comfortable sharing his or her experiences with you.

LEARNING HOW TO LISTEN
When you and your child are having a conversation, listen! When you listen actively, you actually hear things that you would miss if you let your own agenda dominate the conversation.

Certain kinds of parental responses are surefire conversation stoppers. Read the following examples and you'll see how certain responses will inhibit young people from sharing their feelings:

Being judgmental
EXAMPLE: Your daughter is having a difficult time with a certain teacher and is trying to explain to you why she feels she must transfer into another teacher's class. Instead of drawing her out by asking some nonjudgmental questions, you re-

spond in an annoyed tone with a generalizing and judgmental statement such as "Come on, Sharon, quitters are losers. Do you want to be a loser?" The message given by this kind of response is that the parent isn't really listening and has already judged the child in a negative light.

Being self-righteous or hypocritical

EXAMPLE: Your son wants to have a party where beer and cigarettes are allowed. While puffing on a cigarette, you say "No! Absolutely not." Moreover your son has seen you nurse some pretty wicked hangovers, and you and your spouse both have a drink every night.

This kind of response comes under the "do as I say, not as I do" category. Teenagers naturally question their parents values and actions, so they are particularly sensitive to hypocritical and self-righteous behavior on the part of those who still have authority over them.

Criticizing or ridiculing

EXAMPLE: Your son insists on wearing the new haircut that all his friends have. You can't stand it and make this sentiment known by snide comments, such as comparing him to a plucked chicken.

EXAMPLE: Your daughter brings home a bad report card. Instead of listening to her reasons, you instantly start berating her, saying things such as, "If you keep this up, you'll never get into college."

In a time when children are experimenting with their identities and are not quite sure who they are, harsh criticism and ridicule can create a deep alienation between parent and child. It's also important to remember that what some parents might take as teasing will sound cruel to a sensitive adolescent.

Treating the child's problems and concerns lightly
EXAMPLE: Your son has tried out for the school play and didn't even get a minor role. He is devastated and seems depressed. You think this a melodramatic response and say, "Oh, come on, it's just a play. You aren't planning a career in Hollywood are you?"

Understand that something that seems trivial to you may be a big deal for your kid and respect that. Otherwise you may miss something very important going on in your child's life or psyche that will give you clues as to how you can help.

Lecturing your child
Don't assume that your child wants advice. We all know what it is like to have someone continually giving advice but never really listening to it. However, when your child does express a desire for direction, discuss some alternatives.

Listen carefully before offering solutions. Remember that you don't necessarily have all the answers and that your answers are not always relevant. Offer guidance in a few sentences, not a lecture. Remind your child that the door of communication is always open.

LISTEN without judgment. How often do you disapprove of the decisions your child makes in life? You might not like the hair or the clothes, the music or the language, but you must let your child know where you stand without judging. If you play the role of judge, you take the chance that your child will reject your values just to prove that you can't control him or her.

Instead of judging, involve yourself in your child's life as a teacher and guide. Instead of pounding the gavel, address your child's needs, acknowledge what is important to him or her, and always be open to discussion.

Suppose you don't like your daughter's friends and you don't like the fact that she seems to go along with everything they do and say. Be honest about this but talk to her about why it is important for her to start to think and make decisions for herself. Instead of saying negative things about her friends, encourage her to value her individuality.

Effective listening communicates loving concern to your child, but *listening is more than just not talking*. Real listening takes concentration and practice. The five skills below are designed to help even the best parents reach their children.

Listening Skill 1: Rephrase your child's comments to show that you understand. Like everyone else, young people need to sound off about their anger and frustration. When they are upset, they want understanding—not solutions. They will be ready for solutions after they let off steam. One way to sympathize is to answer by rephrasing your child's comments. This is sometimes called reflective listening. Reflective listening serves three purposes: it assures your child that you hear what he or she is saying; it allows your child to rehear and consider his or her own feelings; and it assures you that you correctly understand the child.

EXAMPLE:

CHILD: My math teacher is so mean. He yells at me when I haven't done anything wrong.

PARENT: Do you feel your math teacher is treating you unfairly?

Rather than assuming the child is at fault and saying something such as, "So, what did you do wrong? Were you and your friends fooling around?" this parent opens the door for further communication.

Listening Skill 2: Watch your child's face and body language. Often a child will reassure you that he or she does not feel sad or dejected, but a quivering chin, shifting eyes, or a tightness around the mouth will tell you otherwise. When words and body language say two different things, always believe the body language.

Listening Skill 3: Give nonverbal support and encouragement. This may include giving a smile, a hug, a wink, or a pat on the shoulder, nodding your head, making eye contact, or reaching for your child's hand.

Listening Skill 4: Use the right tone of voice for the answer you are giving. Remember that your voice tone communicates to your child as clearly as your words. Make sure your tone does not come across as sarcastic or all-knowing.

Listening Skill 5: Use encouraging phrases to show your interest and to keep the conversation going. These helpful little phrases spoken during appropriate pauses in conversation can communicate to your child how much you care: "Oh, really?" "Tell me about it." "It sounds as if you..." "Then what happened?"

The following sample conversations demonstrate some of these skills.

SON: Hi, Mom.
MOTHER: Hi, dear. How'd it go today?
SON: Well, I'm really bummed out. I can't believe Tony. I stopped by his house on my way home. His mom wasn't home yet, so the first thing he did was take a beer out of the fridge. He gave

one to me and one to Greg. I told him I didn't
want it, but he made a nasty crack. So I
poured it down the sink. Then he got mad. I
mean really mad.

MOTHER: I know Tony is your friend, but it
sounds to me as if you're upset because Tony
got mad at you. Am I right?

SON: Yeah. I guess so. Mom, I didn't know what
to do when he gave me the beer.

MOTHER: It sounds as if you were nervous and
confused about how to act. At the moment it
was happening you simply reacted quickly.
Now that you can think it over can you try to
come up with another way you might have
handled it?

Other problems might have to be ferreted out.
For example:

MOTHER: Hi. You're home early aren't you?

DAUGHTER: Hi. I guess so.

MOTHER: Anything special happen today? You
seem a little low or am I wrong?

DAUGHTER: Not really. Pam and Elaine keep
talking about . . . well forget it.

MOTHER: You don't have to tell me what they're
talking about if you don't want to.

DAUGHTER: Just stupid stuff, but well, I'm not
like them. I guess they think they are more
sophisticated or something. And I don't really

have a boyfriend, so talking about what I'd do
or wouldn't do is—well embarrassing.

MOTHER: You know, having a boyfriend right
now might seem like the most important
thing on earth. I know that. I was once your
age, if you can believe it! But really, sometimes having a boyfriend isn't the answer to
making you a happy person. I'm sure Pam is
the one facing plenty of pressure. You just
remember these are hard times. Health risks
are real and kids forget that they have plenty
of time to get heavily involved with boys.
Am I right?

DAUGHTER: You know, Mom, sometimes just
talking to you is a good thing to do. How did
you know what was bothering me?

Knowing how to communicate is a fundamental tool for coping well with life's challenges. The
feeling that one cannot express oneself, that one
cannot be heard, leads to a lack of self-control
and an inability to trust self and others. Alcohol
and other drugs often "loosen the tongue," give
the illusion that a person is communicating, that
a person is seen and heard. They are a dangerously
tempting alternative to the real thing.

DEVELOPING AND
ENFORCING HOME RULES

Families differ greatly in the ways they set and enforce rules. On the one hand you want to give your children enough freedom to develop a sense of personal responsibility. On the other hand, when they begin doing things that demonstrate a lack of responsibility, there needs to be a way of getting them to change their behavior.

You can't, nor would you want to, watch your teenagers every single moment. As you have probably discovered, adolescents are constantly exploring the limits of their freedom and your control. This is normal. Part of growing to adulthood is seeking and finally gaining independence. Nevertheless, because drugs and alcohol are so readily available, if we want our kids to be safe, we have to help them. This means supervision by setting clear limits and consistent rules, and then enforcing them.

Children will learn responsibility and accountability only if they have something to be responsible and accountable to. Freedom and privileges come with the demonstration of responsibility. As long as your child is following the established rules, he or she should have the freedom to make decisions and choices on his or her own. You need to be there to monitor rules and to reinforce appropriate behavior.

Discipline and love are related. Our children

may not like some rules. They may moan and groan and try to wheedle their way out of doing things a certain way. However, the rules and guidelines that are set for them, if they are reasonable, straightforward, and consistently enforced, will let our children know that they are cared for.

It is the parent's task to let his or her children know that they matter, that they make a difference in others' lives. If people feel valued, they respect themselves, and if young people respect themselves, it is easier for them to face their problems head-on and reject easier solutions.

In families where parents are divorced, it is helpful if both parents express love and support for the child, no matter what the custody and residential arrangements might be. Contrary to popular belief, research shows that children of divorced parents are no more likely to use drugs and alcohol than children from undivorced families.

Nevertheless, single parents are faced with a special challenge in setting and enforcing rules. If you are a single parent, you may have less time to watch and monitor your child. If you set a rule, it may be harder for you to enforce it because of time constraints and extra pressures. You will probably need to be tougher or get help, to do it effectively. Many communities have parent support groups; or you may be able to call on a family friend or relative to give you some extra support either by talking to your child, if that is appropriate, or simply by lending an ear. Having another person listening and talking, someone to bounce ideas off, can make handling your kids much easier.

Most important, don't let guilt get in the way. Even if you don't have enough time to spend with your child because of work and survival pressures, even if you do drink or smoke, *you have a right and a responsibility to establish and follow through with rules and the consequences of breaking them*.

Be a parent first. Don't try to be a pal. Your children may not like what you do—they may even become angry and distant initially—but remember why you are doing it.

Remind yourself that the struggle and hurt you may go through enforcing rules now is nothing compared to the struggle and hurt you will go through if your children get involved with drugs and alcohol. Be sure to get support for yourself, and realize that there are thousands of single parents out there with the same worries and fears.

SUGGESTIONS FOR DEVELOPING RULES

When you set rules for your child to follow, consider these guidelines:

Be reasonable. Your expectations need to be reasonable. Make the rules tough enough to address the problem but not so difficult that they are virtually impossible to follow. Make sure the consequences you set are appropriate and enforceable. If need be, make consequences stiffer if violations of rules continue.

Be specific. Rules and consequences need to be clear and easy to understand. They should always be stated in advance. Avoid rules that are vague or that will leave your child uncertain or confused about what you expect. You should include your child in the discussion and agree ahead of time on the consequences of breaking the established rules. Be specific about the use of drugs and alcohol. Some kids feel that alcohol is not as serious an issue as other illicit drugs. Make your concerns clear. For example, if you do not want your child to use drugs, say, "You are never to use drugs or associate with anyone who does. If you do, this is what will happen . . ." It is up to you to come up with a punishment that makes sense for your situation and is as constructive as possible.

For instance, grounding kids or making them drop an activity they really value may get the point across but it could do more harm than good. What will take that activity's place? Consider what else the kids may end up doing with that time. Another response might be to ask a child to actually get involved with some activity— for instance, to do some kind of public service or volunteer work. It is also important to make it clear that things will get worse if rules continue to be violated.

Don't be defensive. Setting rules is the perfect time for your child to try to beat you down. When a child challenges your love or your willingness to trust him or her, don't feel you need to go back on the rules you have just established. If your child argues that all the other kids get to go to parties without chaperons, stay out past midnight, and so on, simply say, "We're talking about not using drugs." Be firm. You do not need to defend yourself or your decisions. You may want to write down the rules you've established and the consequences and punishment you've agreed upon so that you and your child share the final choice.

SUGGESTIONS FOR ENFORCING RULES

Once a rule is broken, then what? Rules are rules only when they are enforced. Here are some suggestions that may help make the enforcement of rules less painful.

Follow through. If you do not follow through on the rules and consequences you have set for your child, you are only asking for trouble later. If your child arrives home after the established time, don't let it slip by just because it's only the first time the rule has been broken. Let your child know that you mean what you say. As you follow through on enforcement the first time a rule is broken, remind your child of the rules and the subsequent consequences that will follow the next time the rule is broken.

Be consistent. Rules should be enforced on a consistent and thorough basis, not just when parents get mad enough. Don't waffle, choosing to overlook a broken rule when it's convenient, blowing up when it's not. Hold strong. Remember the purpose of the rules.

For two-parent families and for parents who are not living together but have joint custody of their children, being consistent means that you agree upon and enforce rules, together. Be sure that you are really communicating with each other so that you can speak with one voice. If the child feels that one of you is a little more permissive than the other, the divide-and-conquer game will start.

Parents need to stick together where their child is concerned. Talk to one another and stay on track. Don't let your child develop the habit of thinking, "I'll ask Dad instead of Mom." Your expectations and disagreements regarding rules must be resolved in private, and it's important that you support each other.

Enforce rules in private. If possible, never punish your child in public, especially in front of his or her friends. Enforcement of rules is much more effective if it is done in private.

Provide a means of earning trust. As you discipline your child, avoid saying things that will cut off communication, love, and trust. Don't

let your child think that all is lost if he or she has slipped up or purposely disregarded the rules. Let your child know that you still expect good things of him or her. If your child has let you down, let your child know exactly what needs to be done to earn back your trust.

Rewards. The other side of discipline is giving rewards and praise when improvement is made. Sometimes criticizing can become a habit, or we forget to give compliments either because it doesn't come as naturally or because we assume that our children know that we appreciate the fact that they are trying harder and doing better. Remember that people who are trying to improve need encouragement.

Never let much time pass without explicitly

telling your child that he or she is improving and doing well at something. In spite of the difficulties, let your child know that he or she is loved and important to you. Parents often assume children know these things, but kids like to hear their parents say them.

Try saying things such as:

- I enjoy being with you.
- I'm glad we're here together.
- I think you're a neat kid.
- I love you.
- You are important to me.

Of course, it is not just words that count. Actions do too. So don't forget to smile, listen, spend time alone with your child, hug your child, and share what is important to you.

Rules without enforcement and love don't make sense. Rules that are conscientiously enforced and followed by love can work miracles.

NURTURING SELF-ESTEEM

Most experts agree that if there is one common denominator among drug users it is low self-esteem. Self-esteem is knowing how to take care of oneself, to be nurturing, respectful, and compassionate with oneself and consequently with others. A person who feels good about himself or herself is much more able to reject the temporary good feelings drugs provide.

How can a parent help a child to feel good about himself or herself? Although a parent might think that just loving a child is enough, there are some other things you can do to help foster your child's confidence and self-image.

Below are seven "esteem-building" skills parents can practice to increase a child's self-esteem.*

1. *Give lots of praise*. Look for achievement, even in small tasks, and praise your child often. You are more likely to get behavior you want when you emphasize the positive, and your praise will help your child feel good.

2. *Praise effort, not just accomplishment*. Let your children know that they don't always have to win. Trying hard and giving their best is much more important than winning. Children need to have their efforts acknowledged and praised. Don't deny that winning feels good, but emphasize it's not the only thing that matters.

3. *Help your child set realistic goals*. If child or parent expects too much, the resulting failure can be a crushing blow.

*Adapted from DHHS Publication No. (ADM)–86 1418, 1987.

Suppose that your son—an average ath-
lete—announces he plans to be the school
quarterback. It might be wise to suggest
that just making the team would be a
wonderful goal and a big honor.

On the other hand, low expectations
can be just as damaging as high ones. If
you give your child the idea that you
don't really expect her to make the
honor roll or become the class presi-
dent, you just may be robbing her of
that extra support and encouragement
she needs to reach her full potential.

4. *Don't compare your child's efforts with
others'*. There will always be other children who are better or worse at a sport
than your child, more or less intelligent,
more or less artistic, and so on. Teach
your child to value his or her individuality. Stress what is special and unique
about your child. Ask your child to identify what he or she thinks are those
strengths, skills, and characteristics that
make him or her special, then give positive reinforcement when your child ex-
hibits those strengths. Suggest areas that
you see as strengths that your child may
take for granted or not recognize at all.

5. *Take responsibility for your own negative feelings*. One constructive way to
share your own negative feelings about a

situation is to use "I messages." "I messages" do not make young people feel they are under attack or that they are intrinsically bad. For instance, don't say, "You are such a slob sometimes! When are you going to learn to put your things where they belong?" Instead, say something like: "Keeping this house neat is important to me. I get upset when you leave your books and clothes all over the place."

The "I message" gives an honest statement of need for change, but it also respects your child's feelings.

6. *Give your child real responsibility*. Young people who have regular duties around the house know that they are doing something important to help out. Today many young people feel useless because they have so few chances to participate in and contribute to a common endeavor.

Teens who have responsibilities and duties inside their family environment learn to see themselves as a useful and important part of a team. Completing their responsibilities and duties also instills a sense of accomplishment. (See pages 18–25 for more advice about setting up rules and responsibilities and making sure they are enforced.)

7. *Show your children you love them*. Hugs, kisses, and saying "I love you" help your child feel good about himself or herself. Children are never too young or old to be told that they are loved and highly valued.

CHAPTER 2

Keeping Drugs Out of Your Child's Life

In the previous chapter different ways to nurture healthy, responsible children and promote strong parent-child ties were discussed. These measures will go far to help your child resist drug use. However, the presence of drugs in your children's environment must be addressed directly. After acknowledging that your children have and will continue to have many opportunities to be tempted by drugs as well as opportunities to use drugs, you must arm yourself and your children with tools to deal with the situations that a drug-filled world inevitably presents. These tools will be the knowledge that helps to eliminate the fear and sense of powerlessness one feels when thinking about the drug problems today.

COPING WITH PEER PRESSURE

Peer group relations are an essential part of growing up. The importance of your child's friends and the strong effect their opinions, ideas, and behavior have on him or her are perfectly natural. In fact, the lack of a strong relationship to a group of friends can be harmful to young people, depriving them of the opportunity to learn how to be a friend, to discover both their differences and their commonality with others. The peer group is a place to experiment with new ideas, test out different values, and generally develop a sense of self separate from parents.

However, the peer group should not replace or eclipse the family. While the family might seem to fade into the background during adolescence, it should remain a steady support, a place where young people can still find nourishment and guidance.

Some psychologists believe that peer pressure becomes the dominant force in a young person's life only when there is a lack of parental attention. If parents have not kept the lines of communication open, their children will go elsewhere for guidance and support. While your children's friends are important and necessary, they are not qualified to counsel your child on the various questions and confusions he or she may face.

Studies show that peer pressure is the foremost trigger for adolescent drug use. The degree of peer influence depends on many factors, and some children are more resistant to it than others. Peer pressure is usually strongest when young people enter a new school or a new grade, or in situations where they are lonely and trying to make new friends. It occurs predictably in particular situations such as parties and when there is a lot of unstructured time.

Since lack of self-esteem is thought by many to be directly related to drug and alcohol use among young people, parents should be especially sensitive to kids going through awkward or difficult times. Young people dealing with divorce, death, financial difficulties, or other forms of distress in their families are at special risk. Getting used to a new step-parent or sibling can also create a lot of stress. Kids in these kinds of troubled situations, *especially* when they have no alternative support systems, tend to be those most likely to succumb to group peer pressure.

One of the crucial ways in which you can help your child is by teaching him or her how to deal with peer pressure.

IDENTIFYING TYPES OF PEER PRESSURE

Peer pressure takes many forms and involves all sorts of topics, from dress to speech to drug use. Think back. Remember your own youth and the anxiety you felt to fit in by dressing a particular way, using or not using particular words, and associating with the right people. Did you feel pressure to smoke and drink to fit in? You will probably remember personal situations that correspond to many of the following examples of peer pressure:

Friendly pressure: being offered something as a part of a friendship ritual or with the expectation that the person making the offer is trying to look out for your comfort and welfare. For instance, a friend might say some of the following things: "Listen, don't be afraid of trying this joint. I know what I am doing and I'll be right here. I really want you to experience this great high. We'll have such a cool time together. And I promise there's nothing to worry about. I'm okay, right? *I'm* together. Smoke this and you'll thank me, I swear."

Friendship, acceptance, and affirmation, so important for the adolescent, and even the preadolescent in some cases, is very seductive.

Ridicule: being made fun of or joked about.

The peer group can be rough on someone who is not conforming. Shaming—through such actions as calling someone a mommy's boy or girl, suggesting that someone is weak, fearful, and childish, or accusing someone of being stupid or (even more devastating) uncool—can be a powerful source of pressure.

Threats: being threatened verbally or with physical violence or with losing your status as a friend or a member of the group. This kind of coercion is not too far beyond ridicule. It takes courage and strength not to succumb to this fear of physical and emotional damage.

Dares: being challenged to do something to show that you have the guts to do it. Imagine a group of young people at a party without supervision. Games and "tests" are often a large part of the social interaction in these situations. Daring a young person to smoke pot, drop acid, or drink an enormous amount of beer, wine, or liquor plays on the young person's need to prove himself or herself—a natural part of the adolescent process.

Silent pressure: feeling the need to participate in something because others are doing it; feeling you'll be left out if you don't participate. A young person's stand against smoking pot or drinking could lead to being excluded by his or her group of friends. For some kids, being excluded is too high a price to pay for saying no.

EVEN as adults we feel these forms of pressure when we deal with salespeople, our superiors at work, our friends and neighbors, and the social group to which we belong.

Conformity is a powerful force. Begin teaching your child about social pressure. You might try to discuss with your child the problems of dealing with pressure in general, then lead into a conversation about his or her peer pressure. Perhaps encourage your child to come up with personal examples of being pressured to do things, or talk about movies or books that deal with this issue. Try to identify each example of pressure as one of the types of pressure listed above.

TEACH YOUR CHILD HOW TO
RESIST PEER PRESSURE

All children know how to say no. They've proved it to you countless times by now. But your child might not know how to say no to his or her friends, who after all, are held in special esteem. So it is helpful to have your child practice saying no as if he or she were talking to friends.

Begin discussing with your child ways of resisting pressure. Here are some examples; you can probably come up with some other ones. When you discuss these issues with your child, set the situation up as a hypothetical one so you and your child feel comfortable.

Say "No." There are hundreds of ways to say no, including saying things such as: "I don't want to." "I'd rather not, thanks." "Leave me alone." Practice these and other ways you and your child can devise.

Give a reason or excuse. What did your child say the last time you asked him or her to pick up the room? Perhaps it was something like "Aw gee, Mom, I told so-and-so that I would come over. I promise I'll do that later." Such delay tactics, when used in the proper way, can work with peers. "I can't right now. I have to go."

Coming up with creative reasons for saying no to offers and pressures to use drugs is certainly within a young person's grasp. Kids have been coming up with excuses since they've been old enough to want to stay up past bedtime. Remind your child of this! Some examples include: "I don't drink." "I don't use that stuff." "I don't like the taste." "I'm allergic." Explain to your child that sometimes being offered something that's bad is really a trap. The best thing to do is openly and directly say, "I just don't."

Leave the situation. Sometimes the easiest thing to do is to get away from the pressure. Tell your child to leave the situation and go talk to someone else if he or she needs to. Advise your child to do whatever is needed in order to get away from the pressure. In the case of parties, you might consider helping your child find a way out by driving him or her to the party; you might agree beforehand to wait nearby while your child checks out if he or she wants to stay. If your child feels the need to leave, you'll be nearby. You can also arrange to have the child call you in fifteen or twenty minutes so you can come back if necessary.

Give the cold shoulder. Silence, changing the subject, and laughing it off are also reasonable ways to respond to an unwelcome offer. Pressure is only pressure when it is taken seriously.

Reversing the pressure. Pressure is a two-way street and sometimes the best defense is a strong offense. For example, if someone says, "You can't be my friend if you don't get drunk with me," your child can try to reverse the pressure by saying, "If you were really my friend, you wouldn't keep pressuring me to get drunk."

You and your child may unconsciously know that these are ways to deal with peer pressure, but you should discuss them. Then think of some situations with your child in which pressure to use drugs is likely to occur. Talk about what might be said or done to deal with peer pressure effectively. Consider acting out some of the situations. You shouldn't feel ridiculous suggesting this to your child. Playacting really helps prepare the person to handle the situation.

Refusing offers to use drugs can be difficult, but it's much easier if children know what to say. Practicing ahead of time can really help your child when he or she faces real-life situations. Help them believe in themselves. Teaching children to value their individuality will strengthen their resolve to resist the pressures. So will discussing the real meaning of friendship with your child. If a child understands that a real friend does not judge you by whether you act like the rest of the crowd or push you to do things that you don't really want to do, then it will not be hard to say no. Ask your child if he or she pressures friends in other areas and knows what putting on the pressure feels like. Ask how friends resist your child's pressure—whether it's wearing the same kind of clothes or liking the same music.

Parents try hard to raise well-behaved children. They try to teach children to be polite, respectful, and agreeable. It is especially important, therefore, for children to understand that it is all right to disagree with others and to stand up for themselves at appropriate times. Children need to know that when an individual or a group is trying to pressure them to drink or smoke, the intelligent response is to say no. It takes maturity to respect oneself enough to be able to do so and this needs to be reinforced by adults.

Acknowledge reality. Let your child know that you understand how tough the pressure can be. Reassure your child that you are there for good or bad, that you'll help in any way, and, most important, that you have faith in him or her.

HANDLING YOUR CHILD'S FRIENDS

Friends have a profound influence on young people, and in many instances, they can be more influential than the family. If your child's friends use alcohol and other drugs, your child is at risk of using them too. Learning how to deal with your child's friends can be an important key to helping your child avoid unhealthy influences that friends may be exerting.

Young people usually pick up the habits and mannerisms of their friends. This isn't necessarily a problem. In fact, it is natural. However, if you want to stay in touch with your child, you have to be attentive to your child's friends.

You may find yourself in one of several situations. First, you may not even know who your child's friends are. You may not know about the development of a new relationship until long after it happens, or you may never see or even hear about most of your child's friends. Second, you may be familiar with your child's friends and disapprove of them, in which case you and your child may be arguing constantly over them. You may find that you are having less influence over your child's choices and interactions with friends than you wish. If you are frustrated, try the following suggestions:

Step 1: Get Information and Know
Your Child's Friends

If you are on good terms with your child, talk about his or her closest friends. Go slowly and encourage your child to talk about his or her friends as often as you can. The best way to keep this kind of communication open is to start when your child is young and to make this an important topic of your daily conversation.

Pay attention to the friends' characteristics. Kids who use drugs come from all kinds of families and backgrounds. If your child is unwilling to talk to you about some of his or her friends, it might be wise for you to pay attention to those friends, though you shouldn't assume that they are drug users. If you find your child is reluctant to talk about certain people, try to observe them directly. If you just ask your children if they are using drugs, you will probably get a denial.

Kids who use drugs have many common observable characteristics. These include:

- Friends who are quite a bit older.
- Friends who seem to be left on their own with little or no supervision.
- Friends who are excessively nice to you or who seem manipulative.
- Friends who are low in motivation toward school and have few positive interests.
- Friends who have observable signs of rebelliousness in their manner or in the way they dress.

These qualities don't guarantee that an adolescent is using drugs; but if they do show up in one or more friends, you might want to take a closer look at the situation. No matter what your suspicions, consider the following suggestions:

- Invite your child's friends to join your family in activities like dinners, picnics, or outings so that you can directly observe them.
- Encourage your child to have friends over to the house when you are there. Don't always send them somewhere else. Be available to drive your child and his or her friends to or from a movie or other activity so as to see and hear their interactions.

If these subtle approaches fail to let you know about your child's friends, more direct approaches are necessary.

For example, you might say, "You spend a lot of time with so-and-so but you never talk about him or her. Since you're such good friends, I'd like to know more about him or her." What you get from this may vary greatly depending on what the friend is like and your own child's involvement with that friend.

You may get enough information from this to help you ask more in the future. You may get nothing at all. You may get answers that are designed to put you off the track and make everything seem all right.

Once you ask the question, you need to listen! Keep asking the questions until you are totally satisfied. Remember: Keep yourself involved with your child's life. Stay in touch.

Step 2: Influence Who Your Child's Friends Are

Suppose you find that your child has a friend whom you suspect of drug use. That is a danger sign that should make you concerned. Or, suppose your child is using drugs and you know that your child's friends are too.

You need to worry now not only about your child, but also about your child's friends, who might undercut your efforts to keep your kid off drugs. It will take consistent effort on your part, but protecting your child from destructive rela-

tionships may be the key to helping your child
stay drug-free. You can do this through supervision, questioning, and restrictions. While it may
be clear that you need to protect your child
from friends exerting a negative influence, how
to accomplish this may not be as clear.

Since friends are so important, eliminating
them will not be easy. Your child would rather
fight than give up an important friend, and if you
ask or insist that they do, it may trigger guilt-
inducing tears or out-and-out defiance. Let's face
it, this can be as difficult a challenge as getting a
child off drugs.

Here are a few ideas about how to deal with
this situation and a few suggestions about things
to avoid:

1. *Teach your child to seek out the right
   kind of friends*. In the end we choose
   our friends because they give us enjoyment or support or allow us to become
   something we want to be. Helping your
   child learn how to pick good friends and
   giving him or her the motivation and
   skills to do so is as important as coming
   down hard when you encounter trouble.

   Try attending a church, or synagogue,
   or a social group where the chance of
   finding non-using friends for your child
   might be better. Attending a religious
   community group does not guarantee

anything, however. Unless you are prepared to help find those friends, new friends may not be easy to come by.

2. *Limit exposure*. Because your child spends so much time out and away from you each day, eliminating the influence of a friend at school may be impossible. But there are rules that can be set about how much access friends can have to your child.

   Establish rules about coming home after school and about spending time in places that are appropriate. Insist on knowing about all social activities, especially when there are not specific plans. Prevent your child from associating with questionable friends if you really feel uncomfortable. Again, the rules must be clear and consistent.

   You will need to be constantly watchful. In most families, such rules are enforced for about a week. After that time, special circumstances or a failure to follow through puts the situation right back where it started.

3. *Encourage time spent with "better" friends*. Your child probably has some friends whom you prefer more than others. Identify them and find ways to encourage your child to be more involved with them. Let your child use your home

as a meeting place for friends so you can
see what goes on.

Talk to your child about what he or
she thinks a good friend is and isn't, and
compare this with your own ideas. A
good way to encourage better friends is
by helping your child to think out what
is and is not important about different
relationships.

HANDLING PARTIES

Parties are important to kids. Being asked to a
party is a sign of acceptance, and kids love
talking about the party the next day. For some
teenagers parties are the most important thing in
their lives, and they count the days until Friday
night. Parties are frequently the place where
teenagers first experiment with alcohol and other
drugs, and parents need to be especially alert
when children begin going to parties. It's a critical
time to prevent the future use of drugs.

There are many things that parents can do to
make parties safer and free from drugs.

IF THE PARTY IS AT YOUR HOUSE
Invitation Only. Make sure that your child is
not inviting the whole school, and find out exactly who is invited. Make it clear to your child
that no one else is to attend. Before the party,

tell your child to tell the guests that alcohol and other drugs are not allowed.

Provide Entertainment. Promote activities and entertainment as diversions from eating and drinking. Kids may expect it to be boring without alcohol, so provide them with another attraction that keeps them entertained. You might consider planning parties with a theme, playing special music, or having games and competitions, such as ping-pong or charades.

Serve Non-Alcoholic Drinks. Non-alcoholic drinks don't have to be soda or juice only. Be creative. Try hot chocolate, mulled cider, or eggnog in the winter, and non-alcoholic piña coladas and fruit punches in the summer. Make sure any alcohol you have at your house is stored safely away and that no one has access to it.

Provide Adequate Supervision. Make sure the party is adequately supervised. Just being in the house is not enough; you must be present at the party, making yourself conspicuous. Supervision must also be provided outside the home. If your party is being held in the backyard at night, make sure it is well lit. Guests should be monitored and kept from sneaking away into parked cars, bushes, and so on. Be aware of people who leave the party and return later. They may have gone somewhere else to use drugs. These people need to be checked out before returning. You might even consider not allowing guests to return once they leave.

Have a Contingency Plan. If drinking or drug use does occur, assume responsibility for the health and safety of your guests. See that anyone who has drank or used an illicit substance is driven home by an adult or allowed to spend the night.

IF THE PARTY IS NOT AT YOUR HOUSE

Check It Out. Never allow your child to attend a party without first finding out the basic facts about it. Who is having the party? Where will it be held? When will it begin and end? What type of party is it going to be? Who else is attending? Who is the designated chaperon? Does your child think that drugs or alcohol will be present? Ask for honest answers, because your child probably does know who does and doesn't do drugs and use alcohol. If there are going to be drugs and alcohol you should not allow your child to attend. Anticipate your child's reaction to this and how you will handle the situation.

Don't feel embarrassed to call the parents of the person giving the party. Be sure to ask what type of supervision and entertainment is planned. Do not be afraid to ask direct questions about whether or not beer, wine, or other alcohol will be served. Know ahead of time exactly where your child is, what he or she is doing, and whom he or she is with. It is not unreasonable for your child to supply you with this information.

Make sure that some of the rules you set in your home deal with parties. Plans to attend parties should be cleared in advance. The phone numbers of parents should be made available to you in case you need to call. Make the consequences of violating party rules clear before your child leaves for any party. You may also want to refer to the section on peer pressure (see page 32–40).

Transportation. Make sure you know how your child is getting to and from the party. Provide for alternatives in case plans don't work out.

Follow Through. Establish a pattern of checking up on your child when he or she returns from a party. Set your alarm if need be for the time your child is supposed to return home. Talk with him or her after each party or date. Hug your kid and be alert to the smell of alcohol. Don't allow your child the opportunity to sneak by without scrutiny. You are not being mean or sneaky by doing this. You are proving how concerned you are as a loving parent.

FINDING ALTERNATIVES TO DRUGS

Adolescents frequently sense a void in their lives. Many feel life is boring and no one cares. Often they realize their parents love them, yet even that does not help them deal with the emptiness. For some teenagers drug use becomes a way to numb the depression, temporari-

ly taking away the pain and uncertainty. Those
who turn to drugs often don't see that when the
drug wears off, so does the temporary happiness.
The drug user is left feeling even more lonely,
empty, and useless.

As a parent you must help your child find
positive alternatives to the social activities of
drug use. Chapter 1 stressed the need to help
children develop self-discipline, self-esteem, communication skills, and a sense of responsibility and
accountability. These essential ingredients for drug-
free children cannot be developed in a vacuum or
through a couple of good conversations. The pressures in your child's world are enormous. Your
effort must be on-going and rooted in everyday
activities. It requires persistence—and, in situations where your community offers few alternatives, it requires creativity and energy.

Here are some suggestions to help you handle
the situation.

Spend as much time as possible with your
child. Make the time together feel like pure
enjoyment. Don't use the time to focus on making your child a better person or giving a lecture. You might go to a movie or shopping.
Playing a sport together, even if you're not pros
at it, is a good way to interact. Give your child
attention rather than material things. Just spending money does not help your child face what to
do with his or her boredom or feelings of
emptiness.

If you are a single parent or if you are part of a working couple, chances are that when you get home from work you are dead tired. As much as you love your child, the last thing you want to do is make the extra effort to keep your child entertained. You certainly deserve time to yourself, but don't forget that your child needs attention from you when you are home. In the long run you will find that it is easier to give as much time as you can to your child each day than it will be to deal with a drug problem once it develops or after it is in full bloom. Schedule time for yourself if possible before you walk in the door. Find time for yourself when your child doesn't need it from you. Try as hard as you can not to take time away from the child who is needy.

Encouraging and participating in group activities and outings with other families or relatives can be helpful and fun. Arrange picnics, volleyball games, hikes, camping trips, visits to museums, and attendance at theatrical or musical performances. Sometimes a trip can turn out to be so much fun that everyone gets energy from it. The benefits of having shared something together are well worth the time you might have spent working or being a "couch potato." It is important to teach your child that you can have fun without spending a lot of money.

Money should not become an excuse, for there are usually free activities available to your family or your child and his or her friends. If not, use your ingenuity. A wonderful alternative is to involve yourself and your child in a project together, either at home or outside of your home. Cleaning up the backyard and planting a garden, making family presents by hand, beginning a writing campaign to your local, state, or federal legislature about an issue you feel is important, or starting an environmental action group in your town or on your block are all possibilities. You and your child might decide you want to learn to draw, decorate cakes, or take yoga. Find out if a nearby school holds evening or weekend classes through a continuing education program.

Encourage your child to participate in groups with a goal or a constructive social purpose. Do some local research or make some phone calls to find out what kind of programs, institutions, and organizations are in your area. Churches, synagogues, social service groups, hospitals, senior citizens groups, retirement homes, soup kitchens, and big brother or big sister programs are usually eager to have volunteers. Encourage your child to volunteer his or her time and talents in an area that's interesting. Perhaps he or she can play guitar at the senior citizens' center or read to youngsters at the hospital. Local theater groups sometimes need stagehands or prop people. This is a good way for young people to discover their uniqueness and learn that they have something valuable to offer. These opportunities also provide safe and challenging experiences outside the family circle. During family outings you may want to consider that you are your child's most important role model. You should let your child see that to have fun one does not have to drink alcohol or smoke cigarettes for an enjoyable time. By seeing how content you are by being together as a family, your child will learn to appreciate the same things you value.

COPING WITH DRUGS AND SEX

It is not within the scope of this guide to discuss adolescent sexual activity or offer advice to parents on how to deal with a child's sex education. However, some studies show that kids start drinking and using other drugs around the time that they begin to experiment sexually. It would be wise for parents to be aware of the normal anxiety children feel as they begin maturing sexually and entering into more intimate relationships.

Parents should consider talking to kids about how drugs relate to intimacy and sexual activity. Some of the points you might want to include in a discussion are detailed below.

Explain to your child that some people take drugs or drink so that they can do something daring or risky that they would not ordinarily do. People who do things under the influence think that they can claim that, "Well, I was just drunk" or "I didn't know what I was doing." Let your child know how important it is that people realize they are responsible for what they do whether or not they are under the influence. Make your child understand that the person who did the misdeed made the choice to take the drug in the first place.

Let your child know that you understand the self-consciousness and scary feelings that arise with maturing sexuality. This might create a moment of discomfort between you and your child, but admit with a smile that you were once a kid too! Address the fact that some kids try to overcome these uneasy feelings with drugs and alcohol. Say that it is the same way that some adults try to bolster their courage—by using drugs or alcohol—and it's wrong for adults too. Kids who get high, have sex with someone, and then say, "I didn't know what I was doing" or "I don't know if anything even happened or not" are fooling only themselves. This is certainly not how two people who feel strongly and positively enough about each other to intimately share their bodies and emotions behave. It is merely irresponsible, immature behavior. And in an age of rampant sexual disease, it is physically, as well as emotionally and psychologically, dangerous. Recent studies show that the number of AIDS cases is rapidly growing in the adolescent community. The importance of facing the AIDS crisis must be stressed, not to frighten your child, but to provide necessary information. Teenagers feel invulnerable and they must be convinced that they are not.

Tell your child in no uncertain terms, "You are responsible for everything you do. You are responsible to yourself and your future. If you get drunk and kill somebody with a car, you are responsible and will pay the consequences. It is the same if you get pregnant, or make someone pregnant, contract a disease or make someone unhappy." It's too late to say "I'm sorry" once it's happened.

DISCUSSING ALCOHOL AND
OTHER DRUGS WITH CHILDREN

Parents might not want to even mention drugs to their kids because they hope they won't ever have to face the problem. Unfortunately, TV, radio, billboards, and advertising in general present the issues and temptations, so it is best for parents to be the ones to inform their children. Parents should try to keep abreast of the outside influences being exerted on children by knowing something about what's "in." Kids know the fads, even if they don't realize they are fads, and become eager to be part of whatever it is that seems new and exciting: Parents should try to have ongoing conversations about movies, TV shows, popular singers, or fashion, so that there's a constant nonthreatening dialogue in the family. Mealtimes together might be a good place for these talks or the time spent getting someplace by car or bus could be used.

It is critical that parents discuss drugs with their kids long before they enter adolescence, even when they don't suspect any involvement. If you talk to your children about drugs early on, they will clearly understand your position that drugs are bad and not to be touched. If you don't tell your kids about what *not* to do they might think it is okay to do it. If you leave drugs out of your conversation with your kids, they might take it as a sign that you don't know much

about the realities of their life. All kids have
heard about drugs, and most will be faced with
the choice of using them. So be sure they hear
how you feel about the issue.

Parents need to provide accurate information
about the effects of drugs and to set forth the
family's rules about drug use by the time the
child reaches age nine or ten. This discussion
should be undertaken with the same care and
seriousness with which discussions about sexuality or religion are conducted.

If you find it hard to talk to your child about
drugs and alcohol, get some help. Talk to a
friend, other parents, or even a drug counselor
about the best way to handle the situation.

It is vital to have a "drug-prevention" talk.
Here are some points that you should include:

1. *Drugs are a health hazard*. Share your
   knowledge of the effects of drugs, being
   as concrete and honest as possible.

   Describe the ways that drugs harm
   people's bodies and hinder their physical performance, whether it's doing gym-
   nastics, playing baseball, playing an in-
   strument, or acting in a play.

   Discuss the dangers that drugs pose to
   your child's mind, and how drug use can
   interfere with his or her judgment, education, and the ability to learn new things.
2. *Drugs can make you feel bad*. It is also

important to be very clear about what drugs can potentially do to your child's relationships and how they can cause depression, feelings of shame, and even turn people into liars. Don't deny that some people might feel good for a short time, but say that the high is so short, it's like eating so much candy that you then get sick and regret it.

Try to think of a positive experience your child has had—something that had a strong impact, or something that was a lot of fun—and tell why and how, if he or she had been using drugs at the time, the situation would have been different. Help him recognize that drugs were totally unnecessary for the enjoyment of the experience.

3. *Drugs are powerful and unpredictable.* Parents should stress the fact that drugs are powerful and can have different effects on different people. Children need to know that even if they think they can handle getting stoned or drunk just for fun every once in a while, the dangers definitely outweigh the fun. This is especially important if there is a history of addiction in your family.

4. *Drugs are illegal.* Let your child know that although drugs are easy to get and many young people use them, they are

nevertheless illegal. Talk about the consequences of breaking the law, being arrested, and having a criminal record. Emphasize how serious this is.

5. *Drugs are not allowed in this family*. Enlist your child's support in drafting a family agreement to keep drugs out of the house and out of your lives. Set out clear rules and clear consequences for their violation. Make sure that it is understood that you will enforce those rules and monitor their enforcement.

While you are talking together, reiterate your love for your child and emphasize that the reason for your concern is that you want your child to reach his or her potential for his or her own sake.

Reassure your child that you will always be available for discussion, guidance, and support, and that you are willing to discuss any pressures, anxieties, or confusion your child may have relating to drug use. Be sure to say that you understand that there is peer pressure, but that it takes the courage you feel your child has to do what is right and best.

6. *Alcohol*. Some adults drink beer, wine, or other liquor. The legal age for drinking is twenty-one. The family rules regarding alcohol must be explained clear-

ly. The drinking habits of both parents
should be mentioned and the rules for
children under the drinking age. This
does not mean you are asking your children for their permission if you do drink;
it is simply a way to respect the child's
sense of sharing family rules and attitudes.

BECOMING A BETTER ROLE MODEL

From birth, children pattern their own actions
and behavior on their parents' actions and
behavior. Most parents have noticed their children using a gesture, a manner of speaking, a
facial expression just like their own. And every
parent has heard, "You do it, why can't I?" Whether you are trying to be or not, you are the
primary and fundamental model for your child's
idea of what a person is supposed to be and how
a person is supposed to act. No matter what we
say, our children will imitate what we *do.*

Studies consistently tell us that children are
more likely to use drugs if their parents smoke
cigarettes, use alcohol, take illicit drugs, use any
substance to help alleviate stress, or impart an
ambivalent or even positive attitude toward drugs.
Children's attitudes toward drugs are *primarily*
shaped by their parents' attitudes. It is important
to take a close look at your own attitudes and
behavior toward drugs and alcohol if you want
to understand how you might be contributing

positively and/or negatively to your child's potential or current attitudes and behavior. Ask yourself the following questions and answer honestly:

- Do I use illicit drugs or abuse legal drugs? If the answer is yes, how often, under what circumstances, and why?
- Do I smoke cigarettes or use any other form of tobacco? How often, when, why? What kind of satisfaction do I get from it?
- How often do I drink?
- Does our family have a history of anyone with an alcohol or drug problem?
- Do I drink coffee because I like the flavor or because I can't get going without it?
- Do I pay attention to the prodrug messages my child receives through television, films, and music? If so, do I simply censor or do I take the time to discuss it?
- What are the subtle messages I give to my kids about drugs? Do I say "I *need*..." or "I *want*..."? Do I associate drugs with pleasure or relief?
- Am I aware of the message I've already consciously or unconsciously given to my child?

Answering these questions may not be easy, and the answers may require some difficult changes in behavior or they might prompt you to ask other, perhaps more difficult questions. You may also want to think about your own parents and their behavior. What was their attitude toward drugs? How much was drinking a part of your childhood family? How much attention did your parents give to you? Keep in mind that you are exploring these questions as much for the well-being of your child as you are for yourself.

Remember that no one is perfect, so don't be discouraged. Forgive yourself for your weaknesses. If you are a step-parent or legal guardian it may feel even harder for you. Look to your strengths first. They are invaluable in honestly identifying and then improving those areas in which you need to change. Remember that you love your child and want a happy, healthy family. You'll find the strength and energy to face what must be done.

PART TWO

Intervention

It will not be easy to do, but to deal effectively with a child who is using drugs, you'll need to face harsh reality. Here are three steps you need to take: First, you must learn the facts. That means knowing how to recognize the physical and behavioral signs of drug use. Second, you must be emotionally able to face the truth. That means overcoming the natural and common tendency to deny the reality of the signs you may see. And third, you must mobilize yourself for action. That means learning how to intervene appropriately and effectively when you do have reason to believe that your son or daughter is using drugs.

CHAPTER 3

Recognizing the Signs of Drug Use

Signs of drug use range from the obvious to the nearly imperceptible. If your daughter comes home from a party with liquor on her breath, a staggering gait, and slurred speech, you'd have no trouble concluding she had been drinking. If you find rolling papers and a stash of marijuana in your son's sock drawer, you can safely assume he has been smoking pot. Don't accept your daughter's plea that it won't happen again, or your son's explanation that it's really his friend's. Deal with reality.

But drug or alcohol use is often not easy to detect. Without direct evidence, how can you distinguish behavior that points to drug use from normal behavior? While you should be careful not to make accusations or jump to conclusions based on flimsy evidence, you should also be aware of the behaviors and situations that are often warning signs of drug use. Taken separately, they might simply be part of normal teenage behavior. But if the indications listed below start adding up, you should take a second look.

PHYSICAL EVIDENCE

The most clear-cut sign of drug use is physical evidence of drugs or drug paraphernalia. If you find drugs anywhere in your child's room or possession, you should assume that he or she is using them. As much as you might want to, do not believe the lies you'll probably hear when you confront your child—that the drugs belong to someone else. The chart on pages 139–149 lists and describes various drugs so that you can learn to recognize them and become familiar with the paraphernalia that accompanies drug use. Here's what to look for:

- Flasks, beer coolers, bar supplies, and other alcohol-related items.
- Cigarette rolling papers, roach clips for holding joints, pipes or water pipes for smoking loose pot or hash, pipe cleaners and small metal screens for use with the pipe, butane lighters.

- Glassine envelopes or glass vials used to hold cocaine or crack, tiny spoons, mirrors, and straws used for snorting coke.
- Needles used for shooting up (injecting) heroin or other drugs.
- Missing household liquor, prescription drugs, and inhalants. Some children first obtain the substances they try from their own homes, and their parents unknowingly become a supplier. Keep tabs on exactly what is in your home that might be a source for potential drug use. This includes everything from prescription drugs and alcohol to spray paint, glue, and aerosol cans.
- Know that breath fresheners can disguise the odor of pot or alcohol on the breath.
- Incense and room deodorants are used to disguise the smell of marijuana smoke.
- Decongestants help clear up the nostrils after cocaine or heroin use has stuffed them up.
- Eyedrops help wash away the redness after smoking pot or drinking heavily.
- Sunglasses worn at odd times of the day may be intended to conceal bloodshot eyes.

PHYSICAL APPEARANCE
Your child's appearance may indicate drug use. Watch for the following:

- Bloodshot eyes can indicate heavy drinking and are especially linked with smoking pot or hash.
- Dilated pupils accompany the use of cocaine and other stimulants and hallucinogens.
- Constricted pupils and watery eyes may be signs of heroin use.
- A stuffy or runny nose results from use of inhalants and cocaine. People who are snorting cocaine will sniff frequently.
- Increased appetite is one of the main effects of pot smoking. Pot usually gives smokers a case of the "munchies" while they're high.
- Decreased appetite accompanies use of inhalants, cocaine, crack, and other stimulants, and hallucinogens.
- Slurred speech is caused by too much alcohol or other depressants.
- Frequent thirst and persistent cough accompany use of marijuana and inhalants.
- Vomiting can be a sign of excessive drinking or of heroin use. Nausea also accompanies the use of hallucinogens, inhalants, narcotics, and many designer drugs.

Other physical signs include deteriorating health and increasing susceptibility to infections, flu, and colds; weight loss (with the use of most drugs except marijuana, which may lead to weight gain); increasingly sloppy hygiene and grooming; poor coordination; and memory lapses.

BEHAVIORAL SIGNS
CHANGE IN FRIENDS

Has your child started to hang out with a different group of friends? What are they like? Does your child bring his or her friends around the house less and less? When kids start to use drugs, they often trade in old friends for new ones who also use drugs. They may become part of the "drug crowd."

Pay attention to the friends your child brings home and those who call on the phone. Does your child introduce them to you? Do they identify themselves when you answer the phone? Or is your child reluctant to have you meet new friends and evasive when you ask about them, knowing you might disapprove?

Many parents of former drug users say that the first inkling they had of their kids' drug use was the new set of friends they brought home. "Probably the first thing I noticed was a change in their friends," said a Southern California mother during a treatment program with her daughter. "When they were younger, all of their friends used to come over to the house. Then the friends changed as they began to use drugs. They had a different attitude, a different way of thinking, a different life. And I saw less and less of the friends."

MOOD SWINGS

Abrupt changes in attitude, flare-ups of temper, and tremendous mood swings are classic signs of drug use. But they are also typical of adolescence, so keep your observations and conclusions in perspective. All adolescents experience mood swings, some of which might be quite drastic. Sometimes these go with falling in and out of love. Sometimes they go with success and failure. Given that adolescence is a time of emotional growth and extreme emotional vulnerability, moodiness is to be expected.

REBELLIOUSNESS AND HOSTILITY

A drug-using child is typically resentful, surly, defensive, antagonistic to authority, angry, hostile, and secretive. Anything a parent says may trigger an outburst.

Remember, however, that rebelliousness is also often part of normal adolescence, as kids begin to separate from parents, establish their own identities, and resist parental control. Watch for *changes* in behavior and *extremes* in behavior. If your cheerful, open, cooperative child grows into a secretive, hostile, uncooperative person, pay attention and watch for other signs—as well as new and unstable friends.

WITHDRAWAL AND SECLUSION

Most adolescents voluntarily spend many hours in solitude. They listen to music, read, write poetry, or just retreat by themselves. If this behavior becomes chronic, affecting their ability to relate to family members, it may be an indication of drug use. An unwillingness to talk may be a reason for parents to be concerned.

It is normal for adolescents to want to spend more time alone than they did when they were younger. After all, this is a time when they are pulling away from parental authority and establishing a separate identity. But drug-using kids take this withdrawal to an extreme. Defensive, guilt-ridden, or belligerent about their drug use, they become secretive. They spend hours locked up in their own room, stop participating in family activities, disappear without explanation with their friends, whisper on the telephone, and evade your questions about their activities or whereabouts. They lose interest in hobbies and drop out of organized activities like after-school sports.

This type of withdrawal may be partly psychological, caused by the reduced self-esteem that substance abusers feel when they develop self-destructive habits. Some of the withdrawal is caused directly by the chemical effects of the drugs ingested. Many drugs have depressant properties: Alcohol is a depressant—after the Friday night high comes the Saturday morning hangover. A marijuana high is often followed by lethargy, and hallucinogens and cocaine keep the user up all night, with sleep made up over the next days.

Kids who show reduced motivation, lowered energy, and diminished self-discipline and self-esteem may be caught up in drug use.

APPEARANCE OF DRUGS IN MUSIC, DRESS, CONVERSATION

Kids who use drugs often bring drug-related words, music, clothes, decoration, jokes, and allusions into their daily lives. They may wear T-shirts with drug images or words printed on them; their taste for rock music may change to a preference for heavy metal with a hard, driving beat. Old posters may be replaced by new ones featuring groups whose lyrics praise drugs. Be aware of the image portrayed by the groups your kids listen to, and be attuned to any changes in your child's tastes.

Always keep these observations in balance. Just because kids are listening to a particular type of music doesn't necessarily mean they are using drugs. Remember that your parents may not have liked your taste in music and clothes when you were growing up either!

But if you notice allusions to drugs entering into your child's conversation, clothing, and music, you should take it at least as an expression of curiosity about and interest in drugs, which calls for a serious conversation between you and your child.

CHRONIC DISHONESTY

Drug use usually requires lying. Defensive and guilty, drug-using children lie regularly to cover their tracks. Often the habit of lying becomes generalized; children begin lying gratuitously about everything, not just their drug use—and not only to their parents but also to teachers and other adults.

A fifteen-year-old from Ohio tells this story: "My mother found a film canister with some pot in it in my dresser. She freaked out. I told her, 'Mom, that's oregano! It's a joke, Mom. I knew you'd be looking through my drawers. It's just to tease you!' She sort of believed me but not completely, so when she was at the store, I hid the pot and put some real oregano in the canister. When she came back, I said, 'Mom, I *really* want you to believe me. Come here—smell this, and then smell the oregano in the spice rack!' So she did, and then she was relieved. I really fooled her."

IRRESPONSIBILITY

Drug use frequently goes hand in hand with irresponsible behavior at home and in school. Children may "forget" to do their chores, break family rules, disappear from the scene when you're counting on them to be there, neglect homework—and then they'll deny it all, find flimsy excuses, or blame others.

DIFFICULTY IN SCHOOL

Studies have shown that drug use may cause a drop in grades. This goes for students whose academic performance had been high before drug use as well as for those who were average students. A's become B's and C's; C's become D's and F's. A U.S. Department of Education study found that students using marijuana were twice as likely to average D's and F's as nonusers. The decline in grades often reverses after drug use ends. In addition, drug-using students frequently neglect homework or hand it in late, and they cut classes more frequently. High school seniors who use drugs are three times more likely to skip school than classmates who do not use drugs.

Why the declining academic performance? Many of the most popular drugs, especially marijuana, erode self-discipline and motivation necessary for learning. According to the National Association on Drug Abuse Problems, "Certain drugs affect concentration, memory, attitude, and other skills needed in the classroom, on the athletic field, and on the job." The Department of Education concurs: "Drug use impairs memory, alertness, and achievement. Drugs erode the capacity of students to perform in school, to think, and to act responsibly."

The common symptoms of the decreased motivation caused by drug use include apathy, a short attention span, dulled emotional responses, impaired judgment, difficulty in learning, and poor memory.

STEALING OR INCREASED BORROWING

Drugs cost money. The disappearance of cash or easy-to-sell items like bikes, cameras, or jewelry may be an indicator of drug use. If your child repeatedly borrows money from you, it may be for drugs; if your child suddenly has more money to spend on clothes or other items, it may be from drug dealing.

Pay attention to how much money your child gets through his or her allowance and any jobs. If you know the new stereo cost a lot more than could have been earned by mowing lawns or delivering newspapers, your child may be selling drugs on the side.

A teenage girl in a drug rehabilitation program confessed: "People usually bought drugs for me, so I really didn't have to worry about money. Sometimes, well occasionally, I did steal money from my mom's handbag. Once I sold my bike which was worth about two hundred dollars for thirty-five dollars so I could buy some beer."

At the rehab center kids were willing to talk about their problems. "Girls who are using drugs go out with older guys," another girl explained. "Probably parents don't even realize that. My parents never knew that all the guys I went out with when I was fourteen and fifteen years old were eighteen and nineteen. Because they had money, they had the drugs. I didn't have to pay for anything. Well, I guess I did. They wanted other things from me. I got my drugs so I didn't care."

SUGGESTIONS

Taken alone, few of these warning signs necessarily indicate drug use. Adolescence is a turbulent time, and behavioral changes may not be drug related. But a combination of several of these signs may create a picture suggesting drug use. Without concrete physical evidence such as the presence of drugs, drug paraphernalia, or obvious intoxication, you can't be sure whether your child is using drugs unless he or she tells you. That's why keeping the lines of communication open is so important, and why confronting your child when you suspect drug use is necessary.

Even if your child is not using drugs or has just experimented with drugs briefly, the presence of warning signs should let you know that *now* is the time when you should be concerned. Drug use may be right around the corner, and you don't want it to become a long-term problem in your home.

CHAPTER 4

When You Think Your Child Is Using Drugs

Just as there's no single strategy or magic formula guaranteed to keep your child from using alcohol or drugs, there's also no sure-fire way to get drug use to stop once it has begun. But many of the techniques and principles that apply to prevention also come into play after drug use has started: fostering good communication, involving yourself in your child's life, being in touch and in charge, promoting coping and problem-solving skills, and providing alternatives to the attractions of drugs.

If you find out that your child is using drugs, you should be prepared to intervene. The aim of intervention is to uncover problems in their incipient stages of development, to stem further deterioration, and to guide children to healing and recovery. As discussed, the actions required of you include:

1. gathering the facts to identify the level of drug use;
2. confronting your child in a reasonable, direct dialogue designed to stop drug use and help him or her cope;
3. promoting recovery by setting and enforcing rules, providing guidance, monitoring, and, if necessary, getting your child into professional treatment.

OVERCOMING DENIAL

Although parents across the country are aware of the threat of drugs, most are inclined to think it applies to *other* children, not their own. Several studies have shown that the percentage of parents who think their children are using drugs is far lower than the percentage of children actually using drugs. This fact indicates that a lot of people are living in the fantasy that "it can't happen to *my* child" and destined to echo the words of the California mother who lamented, "I never saw the signs that were so obvious! I guess I didn't know what to look for. And what I did see I didn't want to admit. I should have known. I should have put it together."

Most parents trust their kids, and when they discover that their children have been using drugs, they're shocked. In some cases there may be no warning signs. But more often, the evidence is staring them in the face, and they don't see it—or don't want to. They don't want to have to ask themselves "What did I do wrong?" Placing blame is not the place to start. The most important issues are helping your child and facing the situation.

Denial is a psychological defense mechanism, an unconscious process that people use when they don't know how to handle a situation or feel helpless. By denying the knowledge that a child is using drugs, parents can ward off feeling the pain, disappointment, and guilt, and the burden of having to face the problem directly. Denial is not consciously deliberate, nor is it always bad; indeed, we'd all have given up hope long ago if we didn't use denial to some extent.

Sometimes denial protects us from a situation we are not ready to deal with. But there are times when it becomes counterproductive. When a child has a problem with drug use, failure to acknowledge it and accept its existence will only delay treatment and worsen the problem.

How can parents avoid letting their denial blind them to evidence of their child's drug use? By recognizing the purposes denial serves (avoidance of the painful feelings of shame, guilt, and anger); by realizing that continued denial may lead to far more pain; by resolving to face head-on the dreaded emotions should your suspicions turn out to be justified; and by keeping in mind that there are plenty of other people in the same situation.

GATHERING INFORMATION

Try to imagine three different situations you might have in your home. In the first, suppose you find out that a friend of your daughter's has just been involved in a drug bust at her high school. While you have seen no evidence of drug use by your daughter—no physical signs, no decline in her grades, no increase in her moodiness or withdrawal into privacy—still, you worry that she may have tried drugs if she is associating with someone who sells them. Should you assume your daughter is using drugs too? Should you give her a good talking-to? Should you search her room for evidence?

Now imagine a second situation. Imagine that you've noticed some changes in your son lately. You think he may be drinking beer at parties. He's inattentive to homework and his grades have dropped a bit. He seems more disobedient and withdrawn at times, and he has a new set of friends you're not exactly thrilled with. You suspect he may be using drugs, but you don't know.

In the third situation, suppose you're putting your son's freshly laundered socks into his dresser drawer when you find a plastic bag filled with marijuana and some pills. What should you do?

Here are three situations in which you have three different sets of information. In the first, you have no reason to believe or suspect your kid is using drugs, but you're aware of the danger and you're worried. In the second, you've seen some signs that your child might be using alcohol and drugs, but you do not know for certain. And in the third, you know your kid is using but not to what extent.

In each case, you must plan a face-to-face dialogue with your child in order to find out whether or to what extent he or she is using drugs. The kind of dialogue called for depends on the situation. If you have no evidence of drug use, try asking your child about it first. If you have good grounds for suspicion, try to find out more before making any accusations. And if you have hard evidence of drug use, you'll have to prepare for a confrontation.

Now let's continue to the next stage of the three hypothetical situations discussed here.

IF YOU'RE WORRIED BUT HAVE NO EVIDENCE
In the first situation, you learned that your daughter's friend had been busted on a drug charge.

Ask yourself: What evidence do you have that your daughter has used drugs?

The answer is: None.

You only know that a friend of hers was allegedly caught selling drugs. Is it fair to infer from that that your daughter is using drugs? In the absence of any other signs of drug use, no.

Should you search her room? Again, in the absence of other signs of drug use, no. She has given you no reason to intrude on her privacy.

In this situation it's inappropriate for you to become angry, challenging, and suspicious toward your daughter. To do so will only alienate her. Your concern, however, is well founded. After all, most kids who use illicit drugs get their start in the company of friends or siblings (and many in the company of their parents, for that matter). You would be wise to use the drug incident involving her friend as an opening for a frank discussion. Hopefully, by now you've already had family discussions about the dangers of drugs and helped prepare your children for entering a drug-filled environment, as outlined in Part One, Prevention. Now is a good time to reinforce those earlier discussions—and an opportunity to find out what your child has to say about drug use at school and among friends.

Your discussion must be a dialogue, not a confrontation. Its purposes are (1) to reestablish open communication on the subject of drugs, (2) to find out about your child's attitude toward and relationship with drugs, and (3) to renew your agreement on family rules and principles about drug use.

Although you may be concerned about possible guilt by association, don't make assumptions, become angry, or accuse. It's unfair and unwarranted. A surefire way to antagonize your child and close off productive discussion is illustrated by the approach below.

INEFFECTIVE:

MOTHER: Alan, I was just talking to Marian Reinhardt and she told me that Mark Knoll was arrested for doing drugs at that party Saturday night. The police picked him up because he couldn't even drive straight. You were at that party weren't you? Did you know he was arrested?

ALAN: Yeah, I know about it, Mom. It was really

dumb for him to do drugs, especially since he
was driving that night.

MOTHER: Well, you were at the same party and
you're friends with Mark. Were you doing
drugs too? Is that what goes on at these parties?

ALAN: Look Mom, some kids do drugs and drink,
but I'm not into that. I can still be friends with
them, but it doesn't mean I have to do everything they do.

MOTHER: I don't want you hanging out with
those derelicts and going to those parties. In
fact, I'm grounding you for the next month.

ALAN: Mom, that's not fair! I told you—*I don't
do drugs!*

This is a concerned parent, but one who isn't
even listening! This is the wrong approach. Alan
is saying (1) he isn't a drug user, and (2) even if
he witnesses drug or alcohol use, he remains
committed to not using them himself. Considering that Alan has given no reason to suggest that
he's lying, this parent is way out of line in
making indirect accusations and punishing him
by restricting his activities just because he
happens to know Mark.

A more productive approach is to use the
discussion to find out what is going on with your
son and his friends. Here's a sample dialogue that
might fit this situation; adapt it to suit your own
circumstances and remain calm.

MORE EFFECTIVE:

MOTHER: Alan, I heard Mark Knoll was arrested Saturday night for doing drugs at a party. You were at that party too, weren't you? Did you know he was arrested?

ALAN: Yeah, it's really a bummer.

MOTHER: Look, I know some kids think it's cool to smoke or drink. Do you do that too?

ALAN: No way, Mom. You know I'm not into that scene.

MOTHER: I know you've told me that before, but I also know how hard it is not to follow the crowd.

ALAN: A lot of my friends do drugs, but they all know it's not for me and they don't hassle me about it.

MOTHER: I am glad to hear that, and your father and I trust you. But I know what peer pressure feels like and we hear so many stories about kids getting roped into trying drugs and then they get hooked on them. The next thing you know they're in all kinds of trouble—getting arrested, even getting killed. It's not that I don't trust you, Alan. I just worry about what's going on.

ALAN: I know, Mom, but really, you don't have any reason to worry. I don't drink or do drugs.

MOTHER: I'm sorry if I seem like a nag, but your father and I just love you so much. We don't want anything bad to happen to you. Alan, you know if things ever get tough we're always here to talk with you. We want you to always be honest and open with us. You're a terrific kid and we're glad that you have such a good head on your shoulders. We really love you, Alan.

In such a dialogue, trust your own instincts and history with your child to tell you how much you can be reassured by his or her responses. If you believe your child is telling the truth, be thankful, give a hug, express your love, and drop the subject.

Alan's parents had obviously been in touch with him about their attitude toward drugs. They can rest a little easier. But they shouldn't let their guard down altogether. Parents must keep the lines of communication open and stay involved in their child's life. The temptations are clearly there, it takes constant vigilance to keep your child committed to fight the drug scene all around.

IF YOU SUSPECT DRUG USE
In the second situation, you've seen some signs that your child might be using drugs, but you have no corroboration. Suppose you approach him in the same way Alan's parents talked to him—showing support, love, and concern, avoiding a suspicious or accusatory tone—and he sits in sullen silence, responds to your questions in

monosyllables, or brushes you off with glib and unconvincing answers.

If his responses don't reassure you or make you feel even more concerned—you have every right to be suspicious—and you should take action. Although it is difficult, your right to preserve the safety of your child supersedes the privacy your child is entitled to in a normal situation. You can and should search his room and his belongings, but not in a violent or hysterical manner.

Many parents are uncomfortable searching a child's room. Most families encourage and respect the privacy of individuals, and granting some privacy is generally positive in that it encourages young people to believe that they are trustworthy and that they have the freedom to act responsibly.

But privacy can be abused if it becomes a cover for hiding illegal activities. If your kid has violated your trust, or if you have sound reasons to suspect drug use, then you have the *responsibility* to find out as much as you can for the sake of your child's future. "Sound reasons" are not always easy to define, but certainly the appearance of drugs or drug paraphernalia would fit the bill, and so might a sufficient number of the signs and symptoms of drug use outlined in Chapter 3. If your child comes home drunk from a party; if you find your daughter and her friend in the kitchen at midnight, their eyes bloodshot, the two of them giggling at nothing and eating everything in sight in an obvious case of the "munchies"; if your son suddenly seems to be spending all his time working out in the gym to develop his muscles and begins showing increased aggressiveness, depression, or hair loss, which are associated with steroid use—you have sound reasons to be highly suspicious and to undertake a search of your child's room.

In addition, it's a good idea to pay close attention to your child's activities and companions away from home. Who is he spending most of his time with? Where is she going and what time is she returning?

If your information gathering produces no evidence, you should still share your concerns with your child. Be sure not to communicate an indictment but express your fears based on the love you have for your child.

IF YOU FIND OUT THAT YOUR CHILD IS USING
The third scenario is the most difficult—you've found pot and pills in your son's dresser drawer.

In this situation, you have all the evidence you need that your child is using drugs, but you don't know to what extent. Once you get over your initial shock and anger, you'll need to gather as much information as you can about the nature and extent of your child's drug use in preparation for a confrontation.

You should have a good guess about what drugs are being used, and when, before confronting your child. You may need to search your child's room, belongings, and places where he or she hangs out. You may want to talk to your child's teachers, to the coach, or to other parents.

- Look for drugs, paraphernalia, and any collection of evidence that would suggest that your child has adopted the drug culture.
- Consider where your son might be getting drugs and how he's paying for them.
- Find out whether your child's teachers have noticed any changes in classroom behavior.
- Talk to the parents of your son's best friends to see whether they have noticed any changes or have any worries or suspicions. Compare notes.
- If your child is involved in sports or extracurricular activities, talk to the coach or teacher who oversees the activities. If you suspect steroid use, try to find out whether other children under the supervision of the same coach are experiencing the same signs you've noticed.

Be reasonable. Don't conduct such an exhaustive examination that you fail to act for lack of an airtight case. Get just enough information to be sure that your child is using and to have some

idea of what and how much. Nothing will alienate your child and sabotage your goal more
quickly than to make accusations without justification.

Once you have assembled all the evidence
you can, plan your confrontation. The dialogue
with your child should be undertaken after careful preparation, in the appropriate frame of mind,
at a time and place most conducive to genuine
communication.

CHAPTER 5

Confronting Your Child

D iscovering that your son or daughter is using drugs, or even having strong evidence *suggesting* that your kid might be using drugs, is traumatic. You may be tempted to lash out in anger. You may want to avoid dealing with the issue at all. Neither course is wise. Instead, you must intervene to stop the drug use. Such a confrontation should be done quickly, but with adequate planning. This is a frightening prospect for most parents, because it involves so many unhappy emotions. Rage and disappointment are to be expected. You're also likely to feel guilty and to ask yourself, "Where did I go wrong?" You'll be confused, wondering how long this drug use has been going on, how frequent and serious it is. You'll resent your child's lying or withdrawal from your confidence. You'll probe your memory for clues you might have missed, hints your child may have dropped. You'll blame yourself for letting it happen, for not knowing sooner. And you'll fear for your child's future. All these conflicting emotions coexist with the love you feel, and the combination could cripple any parent from taking appropriate action. One of your most important tasks in preparing for confrontation is attending to your own emotional needs: dealing with your guilt and anger *before* the confrontation.

HANDLING YOUR EMOTIONS
HANDLING YOUR ANGER

It's deeply distressing for most parents to discover that their children are using drugs, and many will get angry about the situation. Anger is an unpleasant emotion to experience, especially when it is directed at someone we love. People get angry when their expectations are not met, when they are frustrated or kept from achieving their goals, when they are betrayed or insulted. They get angry when their kids use drugs.

It's perfectly all right to feel anger. Problems don't arise from people getting angry, but rather from how they handle their emotion. Some clam up, not talking to anyone, while others lash out at the first person in sight, directing their anger at that person rather than where it belongs. Still others will deny that there is a problem and try to go on as if nothing had happened.

Dealing with anger properly is one way of maintaining good health. Your angry feelings need to be confronted and appropriately released. This is not always easy to do, especially when the person with whom you're angry is your child. One of the most difficult things when you are expressing your anger to a child is to remain fair, and not humiliate or belittle him or her.

Here are some ways you might deal with your anger:

1. *Get away*. You may be so furious that you cannot effectively deal with the situation. Take care of yourself first. Before you do any damage to someone or something, get away. Take a walk. Go for a ride. Lock your door. Talk or yell to yourself. You may need to cry, beat on some pillows, or take some slow, deep breaths—do whatever is necessary to get a grip on yourself. Allow yourself a space of time to work it out and calm down.

2. *Focus on the problem*. Focus on what your child has done, not on who he or she is. Focus on the behavior. Instead of saying, "Johnny, you're a worthless druggie," say, "Johnny, your use of drugs is a worthless

habit." You have every right to hate what
the person is doing, but not to hate the
person.

3. *Listen*. Give your child room to express
his or her own anger. Your child will certainly be angry that he or she has been
discovered. Sometimes we become angry
because we misinterpret what happened
or what someone's intent really is. Just
hear your child out. You may learn something that will help you deal with your
own anger. Ultimately, you want to hold on
to the love you have for each other and let
the anger go.

HANDLING YOUR GUILT

Don't let guilt keep you from acting. Parents
start off trying to raise perfect children; it's
expected of us, and we expect it of ourselves. If
our children fail, we feel personally responsible.

It is not easy but very important to reject the
intense self-blame and guilt that can keep you
from wanting to face reality or can incapacitate
you from taking action.

Don't hold yourself up to a standard of perfec-
tion that is humanly unattainable. Don't attribute
every imperfection of your child to some flaw in
your efforts as a parent (unless, of course, your
own use of drugs or alcohol is setting an example your child is following; if that's the case, your

self-blame may be justified). There is only so much that conscientious parents can do for their kids, only so much effort they can reasonably take to protect children from outside harm, only so many decisions they can make on their kids' behalf. The rest is up to the children and subject to forces far beyond any parent's control.

Keep in mind, too, that although there are many things parents can do to reduce the possibility of drug use, no child is guaranteed a life free of risks. Don't take your child's behavior personally. Instead of thinking in terms of blame, focus on defining problems and finding solutions.

Keep your time spent feeling guilty to a minimum. A little guilt will motivate most people to act; too much guilt will keep them from doing anything. Most important, it can block productive action and stop you from helping your child.

PREPARING FOR THE CONFRONTATION
TIMING

You need to find a time to talk to your child. Pick a time when you and your child can devote the full attention the situation deserves. Don't do it in the morning when everyone is rushing to be somewhere; don't do it late when everyone is tired; don't do it when you're angry, when your child's friends are present, or when your child is intoxicated. But don't wait for the perfect time, either; there isn't one. Plan to do it as soon as possible.

If you discover your child is under the influence of drugs, save the confrontation for a time when it won't be wasted. Send him or her to bed and make it clear that you'll deal with the situation the next day.

COORDINATE WITH YOUR SPOUSE

Parents will be vastly more effective if they are in agreement. Make sure you and your spouse agree on the approach you plan to take and the rules you will set. Nothing will undermine your efforts more certainly than to confuse your child with mixed messages or to allow your child to play the two parents off against each other if one is more permissive than the other.

This is a difficult moment for any parent, but it is especially hard for the single parent who doesn't have a partner to turn to for advice, comfort, or support. The ideal situation would be for parents who are divorced or separated to work together so that the child knows that, on this subject at least, they're united. If you're a single parent and it is feasible for your child's other parent to participate, enlist his or her support. Plan and carry out the confrontation together. Do not use this time for animosity with your ex-spouse. Although it is an easy time to turn against each other, for the sake of the child you both love, concentrate on the child's situation, and try to remedy that.

REHEARSE THE CONFRONTATION

When it is time for you to confront your child, plan your opening lines and have them well rehearsed.

Don't start by saying "How could you do this to us?" You will be much more effective if you do not adopt an accusing or blaming tone. Present the situation as a family problem shared by all. Speak calmly and keep your own emotions in check.

Different children will have different responses. Anticipate and be prepared for the various responses your child is likely to have. In these situations kids can be evasive, sullen, hostile, or silent. They may deny drug use, retaliate with counteraccusations, or try to charm or manipulate you out of your seriousness of purpose. Don't fall for any of it.

They may try to make you feel guilty: "You don't trust me. You don't love me. Besides, *you* drink and smoke."

They may deny the importance of the situation: "Marijuana really isn't that bad for you."

They may use the threat of social alienation: "Everybody drinks a little. No one will accept me if I don't drink." "If you don't let me use drugs, I'm moving out."

They may ridicule you: "That's stupid. This whole thing is stupid."

Be ready for such responses so that you don't get pulled into an argument about details. You don't have to refute everything your child may say to you. Know that you are right. Love your child enough to deal with his or her negative response and keep to your agenda.

THE CONFRONTATION

A confrontation is not a trial in front of a judge and jury. It is a dialogue. Your goal is to find out your child's reasons for using drugs, work out a way to substitute healthier alternatives, and get your child's agreement to end drug use. This is an enormous task but it is possible to achieve. Given the emotional extremes both parents and children feel in this charged contest, it's easier to make mistakes than to do it right.

Here are some guidelines to follow about techniques that work and others that don't and should be avoided:

Dos
- Be honest.
- Be direct, not hostile, humorous, or sarcastic.
- Express your love, support, and empathy.
- Treat your child positively and respectfully.
- Show that you take the matter very seriously.
- Explain why drug use concerns you.
- Find out what's bothering your child.

- Listen to your child, allowing him or her to discuss freely any problems with school, family, or friends.
- Know that you are doing the right thing by facing and confronting your child.

Don'ts
- Don't judge, belittle, blame, or condemn your child.
- Don't yell or get angry.
- Don't lecture or pour on the guilt.
- Don't accuse without facts.
- Don't give up.

Step 1: Expose and Explore the Drug Use

Consider this sample opening approach, and alter it to fit your situation.*

PARENT: Honey, we're concerned about some trouble our family might be facing right now. Lately we've noticed some changes that worry us. We love you and want the best for you. We're wondering if there's anything bothering you. I know there's a lot of drinking at parties among your friends, and that kids in your class are taking drugs. We think you might be drinking or using drugs too. [State the reasons.] Would you like to tell us about what you're

---

*Adapted from Barun, Ken. *Keeping the Children You Love Off Drugs*. Boston: Atlantic Monthly Press, 1987.

doing or not doing? Let's talk about what's going on.

At this point, you'll get an admission, an evasion, or a denial.

If your child admits to using drugs, listen attentively, keep your emotions in check, and try to find out what his or her reasons are, how long he or she has been using, and what drugs are being used. Try not to show your disappointment that what you hoped wasn't true actually is. Be aware that this admission is the beginning of really conquering the problem.

One of the most important ways to counteract drug use is to practice and foster honesty. If your child finds that being honest leads to emotional upheaval and swift punishment, he or she will soon learn to be dishonest. This doesn't mean you have to condone your child's drug use. You should still make it clear that your child does not have your permission to take drugs.

It's important in this talk to express your love and empathy. That point can't be repeated too much. Let your child know that you are ready to listen to him or her without condemnation or judgment. As mentioned, the child who is allowed to be heard is the child who is more likely to listen. Following the principles of good communication outlined earlier, talk it through with your son or daughter, allowing him or her to discuss freely any problems in school or with friends. Lend a sympathetic ear to any disclosures about fears and pressures. Share your own vulnerabilities.

Explain why drug use concerns you. Share your knowledge of the effects of drugs, reiterating the dangers to health and intellectual development.

Try to find out why your child began using the substance. What were the circumstances? How did he or she feel? What friends were there? Was pressure applied? Hear out your child without blaming, crying, or getting hysterical.

If your child denies using drugs or evades your questions, tell him or her as calmly as possible why you suspect drug use and reiterate that you're not there to blame or judge but to explore ways to alleviate a problem that concerns the whole family. Reiterate the need for honesty and trust.

If you have direct evidence of drug use, say so. Prepare yourself for a song-and-dance routine but avoid arguing with your child. It is doubtful that you will make the child agree with you. The arguments will only lead to more conflict. The point is not to totally alienate your child, but to present yourself as in control and eager to help.

Don't back down. Most of your child's reactions can be answered starting with one word: "Nevertheless..." If your child says, "But it's not that bad for you," respond with "Nevertheless, you are not allowed to use marijuana." If you have enough information to truly believe your child is using drugs, don't be persuaded to abandon your belief by any "evidence" the child may give to the contrary.

If you're persistent, reasonable, and caring, you should eventually be able to resolve impasses and get back in touch and in charge, which is where you need to be to rectify the situation.

What If Your Kid Won't Talk?

You've probably seen this before...the arms are folded across the chest, and the head is down. Silence. There is an invisible wall between you and your child. You may both be too uncomfortable to share your thoughts. The silence lingers, heavy and menacing.

The communication patterns that you have set with your child have a long history. Even if the doors of communication have been totally open in the past, there may be times when silence overwhelms your attempt to discuss something with your child.

Don't be fooled. Silence is a form of communication. It sometimes occurs when a person believes that what he has to say won't be heard, understood, or respected. It may also occur when the other person knows that what each of you believes is different. To the child who suspects that you are going to challenge those beliefs, silence may be the chosen method of defense.

In such situations, when the point is pushed too far, silence often erupts into anger. This isn't much better. What is needed is a way around the silence that allows both parent and child to open up and ultimately to resolve their differences.

Utilizing some of the techniques below may help to overcome the silence and help communication with your child.

1. Say you will listen without judgment, and keep your word. Make a commitment to truly listen for the entire time your child is talking. Wait until he or she is finished before you respond. Children will talk when they believe that they will be heard. Instead of taking each moment to insert your opinions or to contradict, wait and listen.

2. Let down your own defenses, but not your determination to get to the truth. Ask a question of your child that will allow him or her to get on an even footing with you. Invite your child to challenge your authority. For example, try asking something such as, "Do you think I treat you fairly?" Real-

ize beforehand that you may not like or agree with the response. When your child responds, even if you feel insulted, *don't overreact*. Remain calm and ask your child to define what would make things better. Try to keep your voice calm and even.

3. Guess what your child is thinking. If you talk to your child and there is no response and you feel that you are not getting through, ask yourself, "What would Tom say to me if I allowed him to open up totally and let me know what he is thinking?" Then, with your child's permission, venture to fill in his thoughts. Watch his face as you present your scenario. See if what you think seems to be on target. If you can't judge the response ask questions.

4. Be open-minded. Keep in mind that each child is an individual. Don't have preconceived ideas about what your child is going to say or how he or she might act. Don't assume anything. Let your child know that you want and need to know what he or she is thinking.

5. Look for hidden agendas. When your child is talking, listen for the hidden meaning behind what is said. Your child may be asking for your help in a roundabout way. Questions that ask about what you think of another's behavior or how you would react

to hypothetical situations might be your child's way of wanting to talk without being threatened. Understand that sometimes a child doesn't know how or is afraid to ask directly for help.

6. Ask for opinions. Use open-ended questions to get responses from your child. Avoid asking questions that require only yes and no answers.

7. Be patient. If none of the above techniques cracks the ice, be patient. Keep talking. Gently explain that you will both stay in the room for the sake of trying to deal with the situation. Offer positive comments, making sure that you are sincere. Let your child know that you miss talking with him or her. Give your child a hug or just a friendly hand on the shoulder, and explain that as a parent, even if your child believes you've made mistakes, you are now going to communicate.

Most important, respect your child's right to take time to think about how he or she feels. Let your child know that you can wait for a response without hitting the ceiling or handing out a punishment or physical abuse.

This is a difficult situation and you must brace yourself to use every ounce of patience you have.

Step 2: Set and Enforce Rules
Make it very clear when setting limits what you
expect your child to do. Let your child know
what you expect, what you will allow, and what
you will not allow. "I expect you *never* to use
any drugs, nor to hang around with people who
do." If after you've clearly stated your position,
you find pot in the child's room you might try
this conversation.

MOTHER: Janis, can we talk for a few minutes?

JANIS: Sure, Mom, what's up?

MOTHER: I don't want us to argue, but I did find
   pot in your room when I was cleaning. I
   thought we all understood what the rules are
   about alcohol and drugs, but maybe Dad and I
   haven't been clear enough. Janis, we will
   absolutely not tolerate your using drugs or
   alcohol.

JANIS: But, Mom, that pot's not mine. I was just
   holding it for someone.

MOTHER: What your friends do is their business,
   but you shouldn't be helping them do it.
   Drugs are illegal which makes you an accom-
   plice. But, that's not the issue here. Daddy and
   I feel strongly that using drugs is wrong and
   we don't want you doing them. Janis, we're not
   trying to bombard you with arbitrary rules,
   there are valid reasons why we're against drugs.
   Most important, they're unhealthy, mentally
   and physically. Also, getting high interferes

with your grades, your concentration, your ability to think clearly, your coordination, and even relationships. And of course drugs are illegal.

JANIS: I understand all of that, Mom. But you and Daddy go to parties and drink, so why can't I smoke pot?

MOTHER: It's not illegal for your father and me to drink occasionally. We're responsible adults, not underage, and we never drank or used drugs when we were your age. The choices you make now will affect your whole life. We just want you to become a strong person so you will always be able to resist temptations that come up and might be harmful to you.

JANIS: Mom, I've only tried pot a couple of times. You've blown this totally out of proportion. It's not like I'm addicted or anything.

MOTHER: It doesn't matter how much or how often. The point is you have been using drugs and you're not playing by our rules. We don't want to have to check up on you constantly, but you should know we're prepared to do whatever is necessary to make sure you're not drinking or using drugs. I don't mean to harp on this, but it's only because we care about you and love you so much.

JANIS: I know, Mom. I promise I won't drink or do drugs.

MOTHER: We trusted you, Janis, but you broke that trust. It's going to take a lot of strength and commitment to rebuild that. You said you only tried pot a couple of times, so it shouldn't be hard to stop completely. But you know if you need help, Dad and I are always here for you.

Using whatever words are most comfortable for you, get the message across that you will not tolerate your child's use of drugs. Then follow through. *Do* search his room, check his breath and eyes, call his school. Don't treat your child like a criminal, but do maintain your authority.

In setting rules, expect what is reasonable. Like the rest of us, your child will not be able to become perfect overnight. Unfair expectations put pressures on kids that can prompt them to turn to drugs as a way of dealing with the pressures.

Don't set too high expectations, or your child will live in fear of letting you down, of losing your love if he or she doesn't succeed. Don't set too low expectations; if your child senses that you expect failure, he or she will live up to your expectations. Kids will fail once in a while, and when they do, you should let them express their disappointment and make sure they know they are loved for who they are. Remind your child of his or her strengths, and of the good times you've shared, so that he or she knows that you've always tried to help him or her be happy.

Avoiding the Role of Enabler

Too many parents think of drinking as a teen ritual everyone must go through. Some even go so far as to supply liquor at parties. Their idea is that as long as teens are going to drink, we might as well teach them how to "drink like a man." This is a widespread and dangerous practice.

Underage drinking is illegal, and that message needs to be driven home if it is to have any chance of counteracting all the magazine and television ads in which the liquor industry is telling adolescents how cool it is to drink.

Suppose your child comes home drunk from a party at his friend Todd's house. It will do little good to yell at your child when he walks in drunk. Try saying something like this to him the next morning:

PARENT: Alan, I realize your friends are pressuring you to do what they do. But it's not okay to go along with the crowd where drinking is involved. What they are doing is wrong. It doesn't make you a big man to get drunk. No matter what TV, movies, or ads try to do to convince you that it does. Those things don't count because TV, movies, and ads don't care about you, they care about making money. I care about you. It's against the law for a person your age to drink. You might not care, but I do. It violates our rules as well. I don't want to have to say this more than once. Last night you were in no shape to listen. Now you are sober, so listen. You're not to drink. And you're never to get into a car with someone driving who's been drinking. I want you alive not dead. Call me instead, or call a taxi. You think it can't happen to you, but car accidents with teenage drunken drivers are common. You're going to get mad at me but you should be angry at yourself. You are grounded for what happened last night. You're never going to another party at Todd's house. I've called his parents and told them why. It doesn't make you a baby to act like a responsible person. Show the others what's right. You were lucky this time.

Step 3: Specify Ways to Rebuild Trust

Part of setting and enforcing rules after a trust between parent and child has been broken is to specify concrete ways your child can earn back your trust—and to give  a pat on the back when he or she does them. If a child doesn't see a way of working out the problem and regaining trust, a sense of futility may set in. So when your son or daughter meets reasonable expectations and goals, give some praise and make it clear he or she is earning your trust back.

The Family Contract
In *Keeping the Children You Love Off Drugs*,*
author Ken Barun, a former drug addict himself,
suggests that families write contracts setting out
the rules for children to follow after drug use has
been discovered and confronted. These rules
include the following:

- No use of alcohol or drugs, ever
- No tobacco
- No associating with known drug users
- Obeying all school regulations and remaining on school grounds during the day
- Returning directly home from school
- No going out school nights, unless approved by parents
- Completing all homework and showing it to parents; parents in turn will promise to assist as asked
- No parties without adult supervision; no parties at homes of children unknown to parents
- All phone callers must identify themselves to parents
- Weekend curfews of 10 P.M. for twelve- to fourteen-year-olds; midnight for fifteen- and sixteen-year-olds; and 1 A.M. for seventeen- and eighteen-year-olds.

*Barun, Ken. *Keeping the Children You Love Off Drugs*.
Boston: Atlantic Monthly Press, 1987

AFTER THE CONFRONTATION
MONITORING

Whatever rules your family sets, be certain to monitor your child's behavior closely for at least a month. If he or she adheres to them, you can consider allowing more flexibility.

It may be difficult for you to feel at ease monitoring your child's activities. Don't think of yourself as a cop; you are a concerned parent who is helping your child reestablish his or her equilibrium.

Here's an example of a positive way to monitor activities and lay down the law while treating your child honestly and respectfully.

FATHER: Hey Tim, doesn't the dance start at seven? It's already six-thirty. Sarah's going to be waiting.

TIM: I know. I know. I'm outta here.

FATHER: Whoa! Before you rush out, what time did you say you'd be home?

TIM: Well, it's hard to say. Probably pretty late, so don't wait up.

FATHER: How come? I thought the dance ends at ten?

TIM: It does, but we're all going to Dave's party afterward.

FATHER: Wait a minute. This is the first I've heard of a party. You know you're supposed to tell us ahead of time when you're going to one.

TIM: I know Dad, but this just came up this afternoon.

FATHER: Tim, the rules we discussed are meant to be followed. Who is Dave anyway? Are you a friend of his?

TIM: Not really, but Sarah sort of knows him. Everyone's going to be there, Dad.

FATHER: Does "everyone" include his parents? I don't understand why you'd go to a party at a stranger's home. Why don't you and Sarah and some friends come back here after the dance?

TIM: Dad, get real. Why do you always have to hassle me? Nobody else's parents mind. Come on, I'm going to be late!

FATHER: Look, I'm not concerned about how your friends' parents handle things, I'm concerned about you. I know you're late, but maybe we should go over the rules again. First, we want to know ahead of time about all parties; second, we don't want you going to strangers' houses; third, if you go to a party the parents must be home; and fourth, we don't want you at any parties where drugs and alcohol are present. Tim, we know you have good sense to choose the right parties to go to. And we trust you to follow the rules.

TIM: I will, Dad, I promise. I've got to go now!

FATHER: Okay, Tim, but I expect you home right after the dance.

TIM: But Dad . . .

FATHER: No buts. It's simple. This party goes against all of the rules and you cannot go. I know it doesn't seem fair, but if you play by the rules there won't be any problems.

Expect resistance, resentment, and hostility during a time when you're restricting and monitoring your child's activities. But don't back down. You love your child and are acting in his or her best interest. You need to be the parent, not the best friend. You need to stay in touch and in charge. And you need to be vigilant. Don't lose your temper or raise your voice if you can possibly help it. Don't call your child names or point to his lack of responsibility. State the rules, show your love, and insist that the rules be followed.

HELPING YOUR CHILD COPE WITHOUT DRUGS

Stopping drug use is a delicate time for children who have turned to drugs to help them cope with stress. Children who are first-time experimenters may indeed be able to stop without much difficulty. Children who are regular users will need close supervision and perhaps professional treatment (discussed below) if they are to have any chance at success. Particularly vulnerable are intermittent drug users, whose use has fluctuated with changing circumstances and levels of stress.

It's important to be attentive to any circumstances that might indicate a time of special vulnerability for your child: perhaps you've recently moved to a new place and your child needs to find a new set of friends; or you or your spouse may be under emotional stress that is seeping into your family relationships; or your family is having financial problems and a change of lifestyle; or your child may be having difficulties with friends or teachers at school; or perhaps peer group pressure is intense. These are some of the situations that add up to danger for your child and increase the likelihood that he or she will be tempted to turn back to drugs.

Stay in close touch with your child, and show your willingness to talk about these issues. If necessary, review techniques for dealing with peer group pressure outlined earlier (see page 32–40). Show your child—through your example and through repeated conversations—healthy ways to cope with stress. Here's an example you might find helpful.

MOTHER: Janie, you're awfully quiet. Is everything okay?

JANIE: Hmm, yeah, I guess.

MOTHER: Well, that doesn't sound too convincing. How about a walk? It'll give us some time to talk.

JANIE: Sure. I don't know, Mom. Lately it just seems like everything is going wrong.

MOTHER: What do you mean, honey, at school?

JANIE: That's definitely part of it. School, friends, Rob—just life in general. Sometimes I just wish I could get away from it all.

MOTHER: I know it's rough, but you can't escape. Some people try to, when they're really stressed out, by drinking or taking drugs, but doing that only exacerbates the problems—it doesn't solve anything. You do have to deal with your life. You'll always have to face challenges and situations that are difficult and sometimes unpleasant—we all do. And sometimes, just one problem can make everything else in your life feel unsettled. That's why it's important to talk through each issue in order to keep everything in perspective.

JANIE: I know. But how does just talking about things make you feel better? Talking doesn't necessarily change things.

MOTHER: Talking helps you get to the root of the problem, but you do need to find other ways to cope with your moods and emotions. Don't become a victim of your anger and frustration. You need to find outlets for those feelings. Like at the office today, I wanted to strangle my boss, but I knew I had to deal with the situation and control my feelings. So I went for a nice long walk at lunchtime and that cleared my head. Or sometimes when I come home a bundle of nerves I'll go running to help me relax. Even doing simple things like that gives me a better handle on things.

JANIE: But still, that doesn't change anything. The problems don't go away.

MOTHER: That's true, but believe it or not, even bad days can be learning experiences. The biggest challenges are the ones that help you develop patience and tolerance, and those are important qualities to have in your character.

JANIE: Mom, I'm glad we talked. You always seem to make me feel better.

MOTHER: Good, I'm glad we talked too. You know I'm always here for you and I hope you always feel you can come to me, about anything. These talks help me too, you know.

JANIE: Thanks Mom. I love you.

MOTHER: I love you too.

FORGIVING

Once the incident is over, let go of your anger. Continuing to stay angry does not do anyone any good. Instead, show affection, say "Thanks," and be caring. Your child will eventually come around. Remember, it is impossible to scream or threaten your child into doing what must be done for a long-term remedy.

WHAT KIDS ADVISE PARENTS

In a recent study, sixty high school students were asked how they would handle a child's drug problem if they were parents. Four said they would do nothing. Five answered that they would use physical punishment, commit the child to an institution, or call in the police.

But most respondents stressed discussing the problem with the child. Among the suggestions the teenagers cited:

- Talk in a calm, honest, nonaccusing, adult manner
- Exchange viewpoints
- Find out reasons for the use of drugs
- Be understanding of the young person
- Seek counseling or professional help if necessary
- Find out about the nature and extent of drug use
- Become better informed about drugs
- Explain to the son or daughter the dangers and consequences of use
- Take some disciplinary action, such as imposing restrictions
- Set a good example for children
- See if they are having trouble in school or if something at home is bothering them
- No matter what happens, give love and support

Said one respondent, "You shouldn't yell or scream or say 'Where did I go wrong?' but you should try to understand." Another advised not to "talk to them in a 'See where you went wrong' way, but a 'Let's get better' way."*

DEALING WITH A PERSON UNDER THE INFLUENCE

Have you ever been around someone who is drunk or under the influence of another substance? It's not fun. The person is usually obnoxious, out of control, or unresponsive. You might feel repulsed or disgusted. It's worse when it's your own child.

There may be a time when you have to deal with your teenager while he or she is intoxicated. It may occur one night when your son arrives home after being at a ball game. Your daughter may come home drunk from a date. Your child may be sent home from school after being caught smoking marijuana.

Whatever the specific situation, dealing with an adolescent under the influence of drugs is an important consideration. Be prepared ahead of time to handle this type of situation so you don't get caught off guard.

---

*"Drugs—Use, Misuse, Abuse: Guidance for Families." Hill, Margaret. Published by The Public Affairs Committee, Inc. Public Affairs Pamphlet No. 515A.

Here are some suggestions to consider.

1. *Take care of your child's immediate
   health needs.* Although you may be furious with your child, the first and most
   important thing you need to do is take
   care of any immediate health problems
   such as a rise in temperature, vomiting,
   or headache.

   If your son has consumed a large
   amount of *alcohol* and is unconscious
   or semiconscious, seek immediate medical help. Don't assume he is just drunk.
   Alcohol poisoning can cause severe problems and even death.

   A person under the influence of certain drugs needs particular attention. If
   you suspect that your daughter has been
   taking *barbiturates,* call for medical help
   immediately. Keep her walking to keep
   her conscious. Do *not* give her coffee. If
   you suspect that alcohol and pills have
   also been taken, seek medical help in
   case the stomach needs to be pumped.

   PCP and other hallucinogens have
   unpredictable effects. If you suspect PCP
   use, do not try to talk to your child.
   Instead, get everyone else out of the
   room, cover your child with a blanket,
   and leave him or her alone. Call for
   medical help immediately and report that

you suspect PCP use. If the child is reacting violently, do not attempt to restrain him or her. If your kid has taken LSD, mescaline, or psilocybin, he or she may need soothing and quiet in order to prevent a "bad trip." Seek medical help if the child is in a state of panic. If he or she is not freaking out, put your kid to bed and leave him or her alone until the following day. Check the room occasionally to be sure he or she is sleeping soundly.

2. *Delay confrontation.* As discussed before, attempting to discipline a child under the influence of drugs is not a good idea. You'll probably be upset and your child will not be receptive to what you have to say. Let your child know that you are upset, and that you'll take care of this situation when he or she is sober enough to listen.

3. *Follow through.* Make sure that the next day you follow through on your discipline. Some of your anger may have lessened by morning, but don't let that keep you from confronting your child. Review the above advice on confronting your child, and enforce the rules you've set.

If you have had to enlist medical help, it would be useful to let your family doctor know and set up an appointment

for your child so that your doctor can
talk to him or her about the medical
consequences of drug use. Explain in
advance to your doctor how his or her
help is needed.

CHAPTER 6

Seeking Professional Treatment

Sometimes treating a problem yourself works. Often it doesn't. And while you can't just turn all your problems over to others to solve, trusting professionals to help solve your child's serious problems with drugs is probably a wise idea.

You know you need help when your son or daughter has a regular drug- or alcohol-use habit that has gone on for any extended period of time. Drug dependence is a medical problem and requires professional treatment.

You know you need help when your child has been in trouble with the law or at school because of using drugs or alcohol.

You know you need help when your child

has promised to quit and has not been able to.

Treatment is useful primarily for people who have established drug and alcohol habits. If your child is clearly only in the experimental stage of drug or alcohol use, you may be able to deal with the problem without professional assistance. You should nonetheless be willing to consider treatment if you don't succeed after a reasonable period of time.

Most young people who are experiencing any kind of personal benefit from using drugs will fail to see the negative consequences of using. This includes a denial of addiction as well as a denial that drug use is interfering with living a full and normal life.

Chances are, you will never get your child to admit to you or anyone else that he or she has a

problem. Most young people using drugs regularly will deny it all the more when confronted.

You might want to enlist the help of your family
doctor. If so, tell your child's doctor about the
drug use. Be honest so he or she knows exactly
what's going on with your youngster. The knowl-
edgeable doctor will not prescribe anything with
alcohol or codeine or other addictive drugs.

If you have questions, bring your child to your
doctor. Let the doctor share what he or she
knows about drugs and what they can do to the
mind and body. Sometimes young people will
listen to other adults, especially doctors, more
readily than to their parents.

RESEARCHING THE AVAILABLE RESOURCES

The first step to getting your child into treatment is to find a source of treatment that
you feel you can trust. The following paper was

created by Californians for Drug Free Youth and is a useful checklist of information.

How Do I Choose the Right Treatment Program?

If you ever have to face the problem of deciding what treatment program would be best for someone you know, these guidelines may be helpful.

1. Look for a program that treats substance abuse as well as the individual's underlying personal and family issues.
2. The program should maintain an abstinence contract. Any use is abuse. Effective drug rehabilitation programs believe drug use is a chronic disease.
3. A drug-free environment is essential. It is necessary for the individual to be free of any mood-altering chemicals in order to deal rationally with emotional and behavioral problems. Since most drugs remain in the body tissues for an extended period of time, it is important to allow time to let the influence of the drug subside.
4. Support groups such as AA, NA, CA, ALATEEN, etc., should be incorporated into the treatment program before the individual leaves treatment.
5. Programs should include involvement of and treatment for the whole family. Drug/alcohol addiction is a family dis-

ease because it affects all members of
the family.

6. Choose a local program if a good one
exists in your area. It is critical to the
family and the adolescent going into
treatment that support and contact be
maintained during the treatment phase.
The family unit should remain intact
while working on solutions to the problems associated with drug behavior.

7. Consider the cost of the program. Inpatient programs are more expensive than
outpatient. Check your insurance policy to determine how much they cover.
Most hospitals will assist you on this
matter. If you find that your policy
covers 80%, many treatment facilities
will accept the amount as full coverage.
It pays to ask.

8. Assess the ratio of staff to patients. Ideally the ratio should be no larger than
1 to 6 because staff involvement plays a
major role in the recovery process. A
psychiatrist and/or clinical psychologist
should be on staff for psychotherapy
(group and individual).

9. Since drug use affects every area of the
adolescent's life, good programs assist
in progressively reconstructing each area
of life including family, school, friend-
ships, and leisure-time activities.

10. Ask about the aftercare portion of the program. Many programs have meetings for up to 1 year for patients and family. Aftercare is an important part of any short-term treatment program because the length of time in the hospital is minimal.

11. Successful therapy may be accomplished in either an outpatient or inpatient setting, depending upon the person's needs. With prolonged use, inpatient may be the best alternative. Experimental or recreational users who are motivated may respond equally well to outpatient therapy. Discuss these alternatives with a nonbiased, qualified therapist who has assessed the user's needs.

There are private counselors, hospitals, and service agencies listed in the telephone book under "Alcoholism Information and Treatment" and "Drug Abuse and Addiction Information and Treatment Centers." Listings usually disclose whether or not that program specializes in adolescent drug use. All other information, including mottos and slogans, should be ignored.

At this point you need to be a smart consumer. Drug-use treatment is a business—a very lucrative business. As with any other business, the people who run treatment centers will want to sell you their product. They may discourage you from considering another alternative. Unfortunately, the people who call them are often desperate and are intimidated into going to the first place they call.

As a first step, you should see whether service agencies can help you to evaluate local treatment facilities. There are several toll-free numbers you can call for information about treatment programs. Groups such as the National Institute on Drug Abuse 1-800-729-6686 and 1-800-COCAINE provide information free of charge about what they consider to be effective treatment programs.

Second, check with local hospitals to see what treatment programs they have available or recommend in your area.

While they don't provide treatment services, your school district or church or synagogue may be able to make recommendations about reliable treatment and intervention services. Eliminate treatment that such groups deem unreliable, inappropriate for your circumstances, not affordable, or not reputable.

Treatment is expensive. But it may be the only way to get the help you need. Inpatient care can easily cost $15,000 for one month's treatment. If you don't have insurance that will pick up the cost, you may wish to consider treatment on an outpatient basis.

Outpatient care is obviously less expensive but is still by no means cheap. However, your child's well-being is worth the price. A very few

programs offer scholarships or other price breaks
to disadvantaged families.

After compiling a list of possible treatment
facilities, call or visit each for an interview.
Find out all you can about the cost of the
program, its duration, its treatment methods
and approach. Ask what responsibilities your
child is expected to fulfill and what obliga-
tions and responsibilities the parents have.
Find out whether there are any provisions
for aftercare—transitional monitoring after the
program ends. Your final selection should take
into account the particular problem your child
has, the drugs he or she has been using, and
the personality fit between the organization
and your child.

GETTING YOUR CHILD INTO TREATMENT

Once you have identified a treatment service, your next step is physically getting
your child into treatment. Few children will
go willingly but they cannot be given a choice.

Stories abound about how parents have led,
cajoled, dragged, abducted, and bribed their children into treatment. Try talking to your child
first; it might work. But be sure to have a backup
plan.

If you're married, get your spouse to agree on
a course of action. If you're not married, find a
good friend, preferably one who knows and cares

for your child and whom your child trusts, to help you plan your course of action.

The bottom line is that you must do what you have to do. If you don't get your child into treatment when he or she needs it, you will both continue to suffer—and pay.

Although treatment results don't happen overnight or may seem not to achieve total success in all areas, treatment is vital. Success rates vary widely, depending on such factors as the willingness of the adolescent to enter treatment, the degree of involvement on the part of parents, the depth and duration of the treatment, and the provisions for aftercare. Once your child is in treatment, you can enhance the probability of success by your active involvement and by following the guidelines of the professional staff as strictly as possible.

Treatment in and of itself isn't a cure. Treatment works, but only when parents, and their children, give everything they can give to make it work and follow up with help adjusting to new, drug-free lives at home, in school, and in the community.

AFTERCARE

Follow-up care after treatment is essential. The rate of recidivism following treatment is discouragingly high. This is largely because transitional programs are scarce and because most

children who end treatment go right back to the
same conditions that existed when the problem
arose.

One of the most effective forms of aftercare available is a peer counseling program.
Such programs are not yet widespread, but
many schools and communities have set them
up for children trying to recover from drug
and alcohol problems. Peer group counseling
is a confidential forum in which kids learn
active listening skills and build self-esteem in
an atmosphere of mutual respect. They learn
how to communicate in a controlled environment, how to control their emotions, and how
to talk with their parents. Peer counseling
offers children consistent relationships and

tionships and positive peer pressure where the main focus is the expression of feelings.

You can't take away a dependent user's drugs without putting something back in their place. If your child's class doesn't have a peer counseling program, work with the PTA to start one.

One of the best things you can do is to find or organize a back-up group of parents—ideally, those of your child's best friends. Together, set the same rules. Decide among you which movies and TV programs are appropriate for your kids. Share information about rock performer's lyrics. Forming such a group is a good way to make sure your children are responsibly supervised inside and outside of your home. It can also serve as a workshop for practicing techniques for dealing with children effectively with support and guidance.

Joining a parent group in your community is a rewarding and important choice you should make. You might help serve as a task force that provides information to other parents and lobbies legislators and police to crack down on drug use. There are currently more than 10,000 parent groups across the country.

Parents can do more to stop the epidemic of drug use in our country than any other single group. When parents get together and speak in one voice, it's a voice of authority to be heard loud and clear.

Drugs and Their Effects

Educating yourself about specific drugs is of utmost importance. Not only is it one way of letting your child know that you care enough to be informed, it also enables you to detect any signs of drug use if your child becomes involved.

New information about the effect of drugs is constantly being discovered. Even the drugs themselves are changing. Many experts say that most of the marijuana available today is up to twenty times stronger than it was two decades ago. New drugs, such as the synthetically made "designer drugs," are being developed all the time.

As with so many other facets of adolescent life, drug use is subject to fads; while hallucinogens may be the rage one year, amphetamines might become popular a few years later. Most recently, we have witnessed a dramatic increase in the popularity of "instrumental" drugs—drugs children use for a utilitarian purpose, such as amphetamines for weight loss or steroids for muscle development. According to the National Institute on Drug Abuse, "America's drug epidemic is, in fact, composed of many drug-specific epidemics, and these have not all risen and fallen in unison."

The list that follows summarizes major points about the more commonly used illicit drugs—as well as uncommon ones some children nevertheless encounter. Please note that new street names are introduced constantly, and these names may vary in different parts of the country.

ALCOHOL

Street names: Beer, wine, hard liquor, all advertised brand names.

Drug appearance: Liquid, various colors and flavors.

How used: Drunk.

Immediate effects: Acts as a depressant. Increased body temperature, thirst, loss of motor control and coordination, slurred speech, blurred or double vision, lowered inhibitions, red eyes, puffiness of face.

Long-term effects: Alcoholism, cirrhosis of the liver, heart disease, cell damage to the brain, kidney, and stomach, nutritional deficiencies, shaking, memory loss, sexual dysfunction, fetal alcohol syndrome.

CANNABIS

Marijuana

Street names: Pot, grass, weed, joint, reefer, dope, Acapulco Gold, Mary Jane, Thai sticks, herb, THC, Sinsemilla, Sens.

Drug appearance: Varies. Green, brown, gold, or gray mixture of dried plant leaves, small stems, and flower tops. May come as crumbled dried leaves or dried flower buds on stems. Commonly kept in a clear plastic bag, sometimes in a film canister. Can be loose or rolled into cigarettes ("joints").

How used: Generally rolled in papers and smoked. Sometimes the smoke is inhaled through pipes or the marijuana is cooked in food such as brownies.

Immediate effects: Euphoria, disorientation, excessive laughter, increased respiratory and heart rate, increased appetite. Some smokers become withdrawn, sleepy, and paranoid. Regular pot users often look and function normally. Use of marijuana suppresses the vomiting reflex—when used with alcohol it can cause alcohol poisoning.

Long-term use effects: May affect testosterone levels and sperm count in males. May contain cancer causing agents. May cause psychological addiction. May affect short-term memory and impair learning. May interfere with the menstrual cycle and cause birth defects in babies of heavy users. May interfere with the body's immune response to various infections and diseases. Some studies show that marijuana impairs short-term memory, alters one's sense of time, and reduces the ability to perform tasks requiring concentration, swift reactions, and coordination. In large doses, marijuana may cause visual image distortions and hallucinations.

Hash

Hashish (hash) is a dark green, gray, brown, or black sticky juice that is extracted from the plant and pressed into cakes or slabs that resemble tar or fudge. It is usually kept wrapped in aluminum foil. Small pieces are broken off and smoked in pipes or joints. Hash oil, a tarlike substance, is another extract of the plant. It may be even more potent than marijuana.

INHALANTS (Easily accessible to younger adolescents)

Inhalants include nitrous oxide, amyl nitrite, butyl nitrite, chlorohydrocarbons, and hydrocarbons.

Street names: Laughing gas, whippets, poppers, snappers, rush, bold, locker room, bullet, climax.

Drug appearance: Aerosol paint cans and containers of cleaning fluids contain chlorohydrocarbon vapors that can be inhaled. Glue, gasoline, and paint thinners contain hydrocarbons. Nitrous oxide, or laughing gas, is a popular inhalant that can be obtained in the propellant used in whipped-cream aerosol spray cans. Amyl nitrite is a clear yellowish liquid that comes in ampoules. Butyl nitrite is packaged in small bottles.

How used: Inhaled.

Immediate effects: Induces sneezing, coughing, nosebleeds, lack of coordination, nausea, and loss of appetite. Amyl and butyl nitrite cause headaches, involuntary urination and defecation, and quickened pulse. Large doses may cause disorientation, violence, unconsciousness, suffocation, or death.

Long-term effects: Weight loss, fatigue, potential permanent damage to the nervous system.

COCAINE

Street names: Coke, snow, blow, flake, happy dust, nose candy, super blow, toot, big C, white, lady, snowbirds, speedball (when mixed with heroin).

Drug appearance: White or sometimes yellowish powdery substance that resembles crystalline baking powder. Often sold in small packets of aluminium foil or paper, glassine envelopes, or glass vials—tiny clear or amber glass bottles with screw-on tops.

How used: Snorted, injected, smoked ("freebasing"), absorbed through gums.

Immediate effects: A sense of euphoria, talkativeness, anxiety, excitement, and energy; runny nose; rise in body temperature, blood pressure, heart, and respiratory rate; constriction of blood vessels, dilation of pupils. Effects are short-term, producing an equivalent depressing effect afterward.

Long-term use effects: Psychological and physical addiction, ulceration and deterioration of nasal membranes, paranoid psychosis, hallucinations, cold sweats, convulsions or fainting, respiratory failure, weight loss.

Crack

Street names: Crack, rock smoke.

Drug appearance: Light brown or beige flakes or pellets resembling coagulated soap or cloudy white crystalline pebbles. Usually sold in glass vials or foil pouches.

How used: Smoked in a pipe or crumbled into tobacco or marijuana cigarettes.

Immediate effects: Same as cocaine except more intense and with quicker onset (about ten seconds).

Long-term effects: Lung damage, brain seizures, heart attacks, aggressive and violent behavior. Rapidly addicting.

AMPHETAMINES

Street names: Bennies, black beauties, uppers, whites, speed, dexies, meth.

Drug appearance: Usually in pills and capsules of various shapes, sizes, and colors.

How used: Taken orally. Can be injected.

Immediate effects: Nervousness, hyperactivity, talkativeness, loss of appetite, heavy sweating, sleeplessness followed by long periods of sleep, bright, shiny eyes with dilated pupils.

Long-term use effects: Physically and psychologically addictive. Weight loss is common. Deep depression follows regular use. Users get in a vicious cycle of taking uppers to get high and downers to relax.

DEPRESSANTS

Street names: *Barbiturates:* Barbs, downers, rainbows, reds, yellow jacket, blue or red devils. *Methaqualone:* Quaaludes, ludes, quads. *Tranquilizers:* Valium, Librium, tranqs.

Drug appearance: Usually in tablets and capsules of various shapes, sizes, and colors—most commonly red, yellow, or blue.

How used: Taken orally. Can be injected.

Immediate effects: Calming effect similar to alcohol intoxication, slurred speech, impaired judgment, shallow respiration, uncoordinated gait.

Long-term use effects: Physically and psychologically addictive. Extended use may cause paranoia, personality change, irrationality. When used with alcohol or taken in large doses, convulsions and death may occur. Withdrawal induces restlessness, anxiety, sleeplessness.

HALLUCINOGENS

PCP, Phencyclidine

Street names: Angel dust, dust, duster, monkey dust, sherms, koolies, love boat, lovely, superweed, crystal, killer weed, peace pill, rocket fuel, elephant tranquilizer, supergrass, mist, scuffle, sheets, hog.

Drug appearance: Liquid, capsules, pills, or white crystalline powder.

How used: Smoked, snorted, injected, or taken orally. May also be absorbed through the skin.

Immediate effects: General numbness of hands, face, and legs; rise in respiration, blood pressure, and heart rate; loss of muscle coordination; doubled or blurred vision; flushing or sweating; increased blood flow to smaller blood vessels; jerky eye movements; talkativeness; blocked or incoherent speech; mood changes; bizarre behavior, including possible violence; slowed reaction time; inability to concentrate; euphoria or confusion; hallucinations; time and space distortions; distortion of body image.

Long-term effects: Psychosis, possible PCP flashbacks since it may be stored in fatty tissue and released slowly, permanent brain damage, speech difficulties, short-term memory loss, psychological addiction, mood disorders (depression, anxiety, violent behavior), loss of emotional control.

LSD, Mescaline, Psilocybin

Street names: *LSD:* Acid, orange sunshine, purple haze, paper acid, windowpanes, bad D, green or red dragon, sugar cubes, microdot. *Mescaline:* Mesc. *Psilocybin:* Magic mushrooms.

Drug appearance: Tablets and capsules of various sizes and usually bright colors. Dots on pieces of paper, blotter paper, thin gelatin squares; can be impregnated into stamps, sugar cubes, hard candy, or soda crackers; can be mixed with beverages. Organic peyote buttons are hard brown discs that come from cactus plants. Organic psilocybin is a hallucinogenic mushroom.

How used: Taken orally or may be absorbed through the skin. Peyote buttons are chewed like chewing tobacco, eaten, or smoked. Psilocybin mushrooms are eaten.

Immediate effects: Increased heart rate, body temperature, blood pressure, and blood sugar level; pupil dilation, flushed face; loss of appetite; sleeplessness, exhilaration; time and visual hallucinations, perceived mixing of senses (sight and sound), loss of body image; paranoia, inability to analyze in a structural manner; confusion and loss of emotional control.

Long-term use effects: Flashbacks, chromosomal damage, psychosis, depression.

NARCOTICS

Heroin

Street names: Big H, black tar, brown sugar, caballo, chiva, Chinese red, crap, dope, goods, H, hard stuff, horse, junk, joy powder, Mexican mud, poison, scag, shit, smack, snow, white stuff.

Drug appearance: White, yellowish, or brown powder (depending on origin); tarlike substance; odorless and bitter tasting. Often sold in glassine envelopes or paper or foil packets.

How used: Injected, snorted, or smoked.

Immediate effects: Suppressed central nervous system; nausea and vomiting; constriction of pupils; reduced thirst and hunger; feeling of pulsating euphoria, relief, relaxation, and drowsiness; itchiness. With tolerance or addiction, feelings of the drug effects wear off.

Long-term use effects: Tolerance develops rapidly. Highly addictive. Addiction may lead to malnutrition and hepatitis.

DESIGNER DRUGS

MDMA

Street names: Ecstacy, XTC, Adam, essence.

Drug appearance: White powder, tablets, or capsules.

How used: Taken orally, injected, snorted, or mixed in a beverage.

Immediate effects: MDMA is a synthetic hallucinogen, similar to mescaline. MDMA may lessen inhibitions and cause hallucinations, blurred vision, chills, nausea, sleeplessness, nervousness, and light-headedness.

Long-term use effects: Symptoms similar to amphetamine psychosis may occur: paranoia, anxiety, and delusions.

STEROIDS

Anabolic steroids (*anabolic* means "tissue building"), synthetic variants of male hormones such as testosterone, are normally prescribed for such conditions as asthma and delayed puberty, but most physicians consider it dangerous to prescribe them for healthy teenagers. They are usually obtained through the black market.

Street names: Roids, sauce, juice.

Drug appearance: Usually tablets and capsules of various shapes, sizes, and colors.

How used: Taken orally. Can be injected.

Immediate effects: May lead to aggressive behavior, depression, mania, violence, destructiveness, hair loss, acne.

Long-term use effects: Steroid use is known to cause weight gain and stimulate muscle growth. Side effects have yet to be documented conclusively, but have been linked to stunted growth, acne, breast enlargement in males, temporary infertility, heart problems, deepened voice in females, kidney damage, and liver cancer. About

one-third of users reportedly suffer mild to severe mental disorders (delusions of grandeur,
paranoia, auditory hallucinations, depression, mania), which commonly disappear after use ends
but can cause lasting problems.